ArchiMate® 3.2 Specification

The Open Group Publications available from Van Haren Publishing

The TOGAF® Standard, 10ᵗʰ Edition:
Introduction and Core Concepts
Architecture Development Method
Content, Capability, and Governance
Leader's Guide
ADM Practitioners' Guide
Business Architecture
Enterprise Agility and Digital Transformation
A Pocket Guide

The TOGAF Series:
The TOGAF® Standard, Version 9.2
The TOGAF® Standard, Version 9.2 – A Pocket Guide
TOGAF® 9 Foundation Study Guide, 4th Edition
TOGAF® 9 Certified Study Guide, 4th Edition
TOGAF® Business Architecture Level 1 Study Guide

The Open Group Series:
The IT4IT™ Reference Architecture, Version 3.0
IT4IT™ for Managing the Business of IT – A Management Guide
IT4IT™ Foundation Study Guide, 2nd Edition
The IT4IT™ Reference Architecture, Version 2.1 – A Pocket Guide
Cloud Computing for Business – The Open Group Guide
ArchiMate® 3.1 Specification – A Pocket Guide
ArchiMate® 3.2 Specification
The Digital Practitioner Pocket Guide
The Digital Practitioner Foundation Study Guide
Open Agile Architecture™ – A Standard of The Open Group

The Open Group Press:
The Turning Point: A Novel about Agile Architects Building a Digital Foundation
Managing Digital

The Open Group Security Series:
O-TTPS – A Management Guide
Open Information Security Management Maturity Model (O-ISM3)
Open Enterprise Security Architecture (O-ESA)
Risk Management – The Open Group Guide
The Open FAIR™ Body of Knowledge – A Pocket Guide

All titles are available to purchase from:
www.opengroup.org
www.vanharen.net
and also many international and online distributors.

The Open Group Standard

ArchiMate® 3.2 Specification

Title:	ArchiMate® 3.2 Specification
Series:	The Open Group Series
A Publication of:	The Open Group
Publisher:	Van Haren Publishing, 's-Hertogenbosch, www.vanharen.net
ISBN Paperback:	978 94 018 00955 9
ISBN eBook (pdf):	978 94 018 00956 6
ISBN ePub:	978 94 018 00957 3
Edition:	Seventh edition, first impression, January 2023
Layout:	The Open Group

Document Number: C226

Published by The Open Group, January 2023.

Comments relating to the material contained in this document may be submitted to:
The Open Group
Apex Plaza
Reading
Berkshire, RG1 1AX
United Kingdom

or by electronic mail to: ogspecs@opengroup.org

Contents

List of Figures

List of Examples

List of Tables

Preface

The Open Group

The Open Group is a global consortium that enables the achievement of business objectives through technology standards. With more than 870 member organizations, we have a diverse membership that spans all sectors of the technology community – customers, systems and solutions suppliers, tool vendors, integrators and consultants, as well as academics and researchers.

The mission of The Open Group is to drive the creation of Boundaryless Information Flow™ achieved by:

- Working with customers to capture, understand, and address current and emerging requirements, establish policies, and share best practices

- Working with suppliers, consortia, and standards bodies to develop consensus and facilitate interoperability, to evolve and integrate specifications and open source technologies

- Offering a comprehensive set of services to enhance the operational efficiency of consortia

- Developing and operating the industry's premier certification service and encouraging procurement of certified products

Further information on The Open Group is available at www.opengroup.org.

The Open Group publishes a wide range of technical documentation, most of which is focused on development of Open Group Standards and Guides, but which also includes white papers, technical studies, certification and testing documentation, and business titles. Full details and a catalog are available at www.opengroup.org/library.

This Document

This document is the ArchiMate® 3.2 Specification, a standard of The Open Group. It has been developed and approved by The Open Group.

This edition of the standard includes a number of corrections, clarifications, and improvements to the previous edition, as well as several additions.

Intended Audience

The intended audience of this standard is threefold:

- Those working to shape and implement complex organization change

  Typical job titles include Enterprise Architecture practitioners, Business Architects, IT architects, application architects, data architects, information architects, process architects, infrastructure architects, software architects, systems architects, solutions architects, product/service managers, senior and operational management, project leaders, and anyone working within the reference framework defined by an Enterprise Architecture.

- Those who intend to implement the ArchiMate language in a software tool
  They will find a complete and detailed description of the language in this document.

- The academic community, on which we rely for amending and improving the language based on state-of-the-art research in the architecture field.

Structure

The structure of this standard is as follows:

- Chapter 1, Introduction, provides the introduction to this standard, including the objectives, a brief overview, conformance requirements, and terminology

- Chapter 2, Definitions, defines the general terms used in this standard

- Chapter 3, Language Structure, describes the structure of the ArchiMate modeling language, including the top-level structure, layering, the ArchiMate Core Framework, and the ArchiMate Full Framework

- Chapter 4, Generic Metamodel, describes the structure and elements of the ArchiMate generic metamodel

- Chapter 5, Relationships and Relationship Connectors, describes the relationships in the language

- Chapter 6, Motivation Elements, describes the concepts for expressing the motivation for an architecture, together with examples

- Chapter 7, Strategy Layer, provides elements for modeling the enterprise at a strategic level, together with examples

- Chapter 8, Business Layer, covers the definition and usage of the Business Layer elements, together with examples

- Chapter 9, Application Layer, covers the definition and usage of the Application Layer elements, together with examples

- Chapter 10, Technology Layer, covers the definition and usage of the Technology Layer elements, together with examples

- Chapter 11, Relationships Between Core Layers, covers the relationships between different layers of the language

- Chapter 12, Implementation and Migration Layer, describes the language elements for expressing the implementation and migration aspects of an architecture (e.g., projects, programs, plateaus, and gaps)

- Chapter 13, Stakeholders, Architecture Views, and Viewpoints, describes the ArchiMate viewpoint mechanism

- Chapter 14, Language Customization Mechanisms, describes how to customize the ArchiMate language for specialized or domain-specific purposes

- Appendix A, Summary of Language Notation, is an informative appendix

- Appendix B, Relationships (Normative), is a normative appendix detailing the required relationships between elements of the language and the rules to derive these

- Appendix C, Example Viewpoints, presents a set of architecture viewpoints, developed in ArchiMate notation based on practical experience

  All viewpoints are described in detail. The appendix specifies the elements, relationships, usage guidelines, goals, and target groups for each viewpoint.

- Appendix D, Relationship to Other Standards, Specifications, and Guidance Documents, describes the relationships of the ArchiMate language to other standards and specifications, including the TOGAF® framework, the BIZBOK® Guide, BPMN™, UML®, and BMM™

- Appendix E, Changes from Version 2.1 to Version 3.2, is an informative appendix outlining the changes in the standard between Version 2.1 and Version 3.2

Trademarks

ArchiMate, DirecNet, Making Standards Work, Open O logo, Open O and Check Certification logo, Platform 3.0, The Open Group, TOGAF, UNIX, UNIXWARE, and the Open Brand X logo are registered trademarks and Boundaryless Information Flow, Build with Integrity Buy with Confidence, Commercial Aviation Reference Architecture, Dependability Through Assuredness, Digital Practitioner Body of Knowledge, DPBoK, EMMM, FACE, the FACE logo, FHIM Profile Builder, the FHIM logo, FPB, Future Airborne Capability Environment, IT4IT, the IT4IT logo, O-AA, O-DEF, O-HERA, O-PAS, Open Agile Architecture, Open FAIR, Open Footprint, Open Process Automation, Open Subsurface Data Universe, Open Trusted Technology Provider, OSDU, Sensor Integration Simplified, SOSA, and the SOSA logo are trademarks of The Open Group.

A Guide to the Business Architecture Body of Knowledge and BIZBOK are registered trademarks of the Business Architecture Guild.

Java is a registered trademark of Oracle and/or its affiliates.

UML and Unified Modeling Language are registered trademarks and BMM, BPMN, Business Motivation Model, and Business Process Modeling Notation are trademarks of the Object Management Group.

All other brands, company, and product names are used for identification purposes only and may be trademarks that are the sole property of their respective owners.

Acknowledgements

The Open Group gratefully acknowledges The Open Group ArchiMate Forum for developing this standard.

The Open Group gratefully acknowledges the contribution of the following people in the development of this and earlier versions of this standard:

- Iver Band, EA Principals & Cambia Health Solutions
- Thorbjørn Ellefsen, Capgemini
- William Estrem, Metaplexity Associates
- Maria-Eugenia Iacob, University of Twente
- Henk Jonkers, BiZZdesign
- Marc M. Lankhorst, BiZZdesign
- Dag Nilsen, Biner
- Carlo Poli, Macaw
- Erik (H.A.) Proper, Luxembourg Institute for Science and Technology & Radboud University Nijmegen
- Dick A.C. Quartel, BiZZdesign
- G. Edward Roberts, Elparazim
- Jean-Baptiste Sarrodie, BNP PARIBAS
- Serge Thorn, Metaplexity Fellow

The Open Group gratefully acknowledges the ArchiMate User Community for providing feedback on previous versions of this standard and providing valuable input to The Open Group ArchiMate Forum. The Open Group and ArchiMate project team would like to thank in particular the following individuals for their support and review of this and earlier versions of this standard:

- Adina Aldea
- Mary Beijleveld
- Alexander Bielowski
- Remco de Boer
- Steven Bradley
- Adrian Campbell
- John Coleshaw
- Jörgen Dahlberg
- Garry Doherty
- Ingvar Elmér
- Wilco Engelsman
- Roland Ettema
- Henry M. Franken
- Mats Gejnevall
- David Gilmour
- Sonia González
- Kirk Hansen
- Jos van Hillegersberg
- Judith Jones
- Andrew Josey
- Maria Karancsi

- Neil Kemp
- Ryan Kennedy
- Rolf Knoll
- Louw Labuschagne
- Antoine Lonjon
- Kalin Maldzhanski
- Leos Mates
- Patrick Michels
- Steven Mileham
- Veer Muchandi
- Michelle Nieuwoudt
- Erwin Oord
- Antonio Plais
- Stephane Renaud
- Milan Rubeš
- Daniel Simon
- Sergey Startcev
- Ed Walters
- Gerben Wierda
- Egon Willemsz

The first version of this standard was largely produced by the ArchiMate project. The Open Group gratefully acknowledges the contribution of the many people – former members of the project team – who have contributed to it.

The ArchiMate project comprised the following organizations:

- ABN AMRO
- Centrum voor Wiskunde en Informatica
- Dutch Tax and Customs Administration
- Leiden Institute of Advanced Computer Science
- Novay
- Ordina
- Radboud Universiteit Nijmegen
- Stichting Pensioenfonds ABP

Referenced Documents

The following documents are referenced in this standard. These references are informative.

(Please note that the links below are good at the time of writing but cannot be guaranteed for the future.)

[1]   Enterprise Architecture at Work: Modeling, Communication, and Analysis, Fourth Edition, M.M. Lankhorst et al., Springer, 2016.

[2]   The Anatomy of the ArchiMate® Language, M.M. Lankhorst, H.A. Proper, H. Jonkers, International Journal of Information Systems Modeling and Design (IJISMD), 1(1):1-32, January-March 2010.

[3]   Extending Enterprise Architecture Modeling with Business Goals and Requirements, W. Engelsman, D.A.C. Quartel, H. Jonkers, M.J. van Sinderen, Enterprise Information Systems, 5(1):9-36, 2011.

[4]   TOGAF® Standard, 10th Edition, a standard of The Open Group (C220), April 2022, published by The Open Group; refer to: www.opengroup.org/library/c220.

[5]   Extending and Formalizing the Framework for Information Systems Architecture, J.F. Sowa, J.A. Zachman, IBM Systems Journal, Volume 31, No. 3, pp.590-616, 1992.

[6]   How to Use the ArchiMate® Modeling Language to Support the TOGAF® Standard, The Open Group Guide (G21E), April 2022, published by The Open Group; refer to: www.opengroup.org/library/g21e.

[7]   Unified Modeling Language®: Superstructure, Version 2.0 (formal/05-07-04), Object Management Group, August 2005.

[8]   Unified Modeling Language®: Infrastructure, Version 2.4.1 (formal/201-08-05), Object Management Group, August 2011.

[9]   A Business Process Design Language, H. Eertink, W. Janssen, P. Oude Luttighuis, W. Teeuw, C. Vissers, in Proceedings of the First World Congress on Formal Methods, Toulouse, France, September 1999.

[10]   Enterprise Business Architecture: The Formal Link Between Strategy and Results, R. Whittle, C.B. Myrick, CRC Press, 2004.

[11]   Composition of Relations in Enterprise Architecture, R. van Buuren, H. Jonkers, M.E. Iacob, P. Strating, in Proceedings of the Second International Conference on Graph Transformation, pp.39-53, edited by H. Ehrig et al., Rome, Italy, 2004.

[12]   Business Process Modeling Notation™ (BPMN™), Version 2.0 (formal/2011-01-03), Object Management Group, 2011.

[13]   Performance and Cost Analysis of Service-Oriented Enterprise Architectures, H. Jonkers, M.E. Iacob, in Global Implications of Modern Enterprise Information Systems: Technologies and Applications, edited by A. Gunasekaran, IGI Global, 2009.

[14]   ISO/IEC 42010:2011, Systems and Software Engineering – Recommended Practice for Architectural Description of Software-Intensive Systems, Edition 1.

[15]   Business Motivation Model™ (BMM™), Version 1.1 (formal/2010-05-01), Object Management Group, 2010.

[16]   Using the ArchiMate® Language with UML®, White Paper (W134), September 2013, published by The Open Group; refer to: www.opengroup.org/library/w134.

[17]   TOGAF® Series Guide: Value Streams (G178), April 2022, published by The Open Group: refer to: www.opengroup.org/library/g178.

[18]   Business Architecture Guild. A Guide to the Business Architecture Body of Knowledge® (BIZBOK® Guide), Version 7.0, 2018; refer to: www.businessarchitectureguild.org.

[19]   TOGAF® Series Guide: The TOGAF® Technical Reference Model (TRM) (G175), September 2017, published by The Open Group: refer to: www.opengroup.org/library/g175.

[20]   ArchiMate® Model Exchange File Format for the ArchiMate Modeling Language, Version 3.0, The Open Group Standard (C174), May 2017, published by The Open Group; refer to: www.opengroup.org/library/c174.

[21]   TOGAF® Series Guide: Business Capabilities, Version 2 (G211), April 2022, published by The Open Group; refer to: www.opengroup.org/library/g211.

1 Introduction

1.1 Objective

This standard is the specification of the ArchiMate Enterprise Architecture modeling language, a visual language with a set of default iconography for describing, analyzing, and communicating many concerns of Enterprise Architectures as they change over time. The standard provides a set of entities and relationships with their corresponding iconography for the representation of Architecture Descriptions. The ArchiMate ecosystem also supports an exchange format in XML which allows model and diagram exchange between tools [20].

1.2 Overview

An Enterprise Architecture is typically developed because key people have concerns that need to be addressed by the business and IT systems within an organization. Such people are commonly referred to as the "stakeholders" of the Enterprise Architecture. The role of the architect is to address these concerns by identifying and refining the motivation and strategy expressed by stakeholders, developing an architecture, and creating views of the architecture that show how it addresses and balances stakeholder concerns. Without an Enterprise Architecture, it is unlikely that all concerns and requirements are considered and addressed.

The ArchiMate Enterprise Architecture modeling language provides a uniform representation for diagrams that describe Enterprise Architectures. It includes concepts for specifying inter-related architectures, specific viewpoints for selected stakeholders, and language customization mechanisms. It offers an integrated architectural approach that describes and visualizes different architecture domains and their underlying relations and dependencies. Its language framework provides a structuring mechanism for architecture domains, layers, and aspects. It distinguishes between the model elements and their notation, to allow for varied, stakeholder-oriented depictions of architecture information. The language uses service-orientation to distinguish and relate the Business, Application, and Technology Layers of Enterprise Architectures, and uses realization relationships to relate concrete elements to more abstract elements across these layers.

1.3 Conformance

The ArchiMate language may be implemented in software used for Enterprise Architecture modeling. For the purposes of this standard, the conformance requirements for implementations of the language given in this section apply. A conforming implementation:

1. Shall support the language structure, generic metamodel, relationships, layers, cross-layer dependencies, and other elements as specified in Chapters 3, 4, 5, 6, 7, 8, 9, 10, 11, and 12

2. Shall support the standard iconography as specified in Chapters 4, 5, 6, 7, 8, 9, 10, and 12, and summarized in Appendix A

3. Shall support the viewpoint mechanism as specified in Chapter 13

4. Shall support the language customization mechanisms as specified in Chapter 14 in an implementation-defined manner

5. Shall support the relationships between elements as specified in Appendix B

6. May support the example viewpoints described in Appendix C

Readers are advised to check The Open Group website for additional conformance and certification requirements referencing this standard.

1.4 Normative References

None.

1.5 Terminology

For the purposes of this standard, the following terminology definitions apply:

Can   Describes a possible feature or behavior available to the user.

Deprecated   Items identified as deprecated may be removed in the next version of this standard.

Implementation-defined
                Describes a value or behavior that is not defined by this standard but is selected by an implementor of a software tool. The value or behavior may vary among implementations that conform to this standard. A user should not rely on the existence of the value or behavior. The implementor shall document such a value or behavior so that it can be used correctly by a user.

May   Describes a feature or behavior that is optional. To avoid ambiguity, the opposite of "may" is expressed as "need not", instead of "may not".

Obsolescent Certain features are obsolescent, which means that they may be considered for withdrawal in future versions of this standard. They are retained because of their widespread use, but their use is discouraged.

Shall   Describes a feature or behavior that is a requirement. To avoid ambiguity, do not use "must" as an alternative to "shall".

Shall not   Describes a feature or behavior that is an absolute prohibition.

Should   Describes a feature or behavior that is recommended but not required.

Will   Same meaning as "shall"; "shall" is the preferred term.

1.6 Future Directions

None.

2 Definitions

For the purposes of this standard, the following terms and definitions apply. The TOGAF®
framework [4] should be referenced for Enterprise Architecture-related terms not defined in this
chapter. Merriam-Webster's Collegiate Dictionary (11th Edition) should be referenced for all other
terms not defined in this chapter.

Any conflict between definitions described here and the TOGAF framework is unintentional. If
the definition of a term is specific to the ArchiMate modeling language, and a general definition
is defined by the TOGAF framework, then this is noted in the definition.

2.1 ArchiMate Core Framework

A reference structure used to classify elements of the ArchiMate core language. It consists of three
layers and three aspects.

Note: The ArchiMate Core Framework is defined in detail in Section 3.4.

2.2 ArchiMate Core Language

The central part of the ArchiMate language that defines the concepts to model Enterprise
Architectures. It includes concepts from three layers: Business, Application, and Technology
(including Physical).

2.3 Architecture View

A representation of a system from the perspective of a related set of concerns.

Note: In some sections of this standard, the term "view" is used as a synonym for "architecture
view".

2.4 Architecture Viewpoint

A specification of the conventions for a particular kind of architecture view.

Note: In some sections of this standard, the term "viewpoint" is used as a synonym for
"architecture viewpoint".

2.5 Aspect

Classification of elements based on layer-independent characteristics related to the concerns of
different stakeholders. Used for positioning elements in the ArchiMate metamodel. See also
Section 2.9.

Note: Aspects are described in Section 3.4.

2.6 Attribute

A property associated with an ArchiMate language element or relationship.

2.7 Composite Element

An element consisting of other elements from multiple aspects or layers of the language.

2.8 Concept

Either an element, a relationship, or a relationship connector. See also Section 2.12 and Section 2.14.

Note: The top-level language structure is defined in detail in Section 3.2.

2.9 Conformance

Fulfillment of specified requirements.

2.10 Conforming Implementation

An implementation which satisfies the conformance requirements defined by the conformance clause of this standard. See Section 1.3.

2.11 Core Element

A structure or behavior element in one of the core layers of the ArchiMate language.

Note: Core elements are described in detail in Section 3.4.

2.12 Element

Basic unit in the ArchiMate metamodel. Used to define and describe the constituent parts of Enterprise Architectures and their unique set of characteristics.

2.13 Layer

An abstraction of the ArchiMate framework at which an enterprise can be modeled.

2.14 Model

A collection of concepts in the context of the ArchiMate language structure.

Note: The top-level language structure is defined in detail in Section 3.2.

For a general definition of model, see the TOGAF framework [4].

2.15 Relationship

A connection between a source and target concept. Classified as structural, dependency, dynamic, or other.

Note: Relationships are defined in detail in Chapter 5.

2.16 Relationship Connector

A concept that connects two or more relationships of the same type.

3　Language Structure

This chapter describes the structure of the ArchiMate Enterprise Architecture modeling language. The detailed definition and examples of its standard set of elements and relationships follow in Chapter 4 to Chapter 12.

3.1　Language Design Considerations

A key challenge in the development of a general metamodel for Enterprise Architecture is to strike a balance between the specificity of languages for individual architecture domains and a very general set of architecture concepts, which reflects a view of systems as a mere set of inter-related entities.

The design of the ArchiMate language started from a set of relatively generic concepts. These have been specialized towards application at different architectural layers, as explained in the following sections. The most important design restriction on the language is that it has been explicitly designed to be as small as possible, but still usable for most Enterprise Architecture modeling tasks. Many other languages try to accommodate the needs of all possible users. In the interest of simplicity of learning and use, the ArchiMate language has been limited to the concepts that suffice for modeling the proverbial 80% of practical cases.

This standard does not describe the detailed rationale behind the design of the ArchiMate language. The interested reader is referred to [1], [2], and [3], which provide a detailed description of the language construction and design considerations.

3.2　Top-Level Language Structure

Figure 1 outlines the top-level hierarchical structure of the language:

- A model is a collection of *concepts* – a concept is either an *element* or a *relationship*

- An element is either a behavior element, a structure element, a motivation element, or a composite element

Note that these are *abstract* concepts; they are not intended to be used directly in models. To signify this, they are depicted in white with labels in italics. See Chapter 4 for an explanation of the notation used in Figure 1.

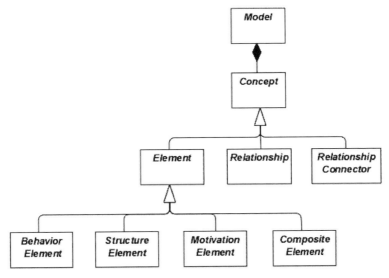

Figure 1: Top-Level Hierarchy of ArchiMate Concepts

3.3 Layering of the ArchiMate Language

The ArchiMate core language defines a structure of generic elements and their relationships, which can be specialized in different layers. Three layers are defined within the ArchiMate core language as follows:

1. The *Business Layer* depicts business services offered to customers, which are realized in the organization by business processes performed by business actors.

2. The *Application Layer* depicts application services that support the business, and the applications that realize them.

3. The *Technology Layer* comprises both information and operational technology. You can model, for example, processing, storage, and communication technology in support of the application world and Business Layers, and model operational or physical technology with facilities, physical equipment, materials, and distribution networks.

The general structure of models within the different layers is similar. The same types of elements and relationships are used, although their exact nature and granularity differ. In the next chapter, the structure of the generic metamodel is presented. In Chapter 8, Chapter 9, and Chapter 10 these elements are specialized to obtain elements specific to a particular layer.

In alignment with service-orientation, the most important relationship between layers is formed by "serving"[1] relationships, which show how the elements in one layer are served by the services of other layers. (Note, however, that services need not only serve elements in another layer, but also can serve elements in the same layer.) A second type of link is formed by realization relationships: elements in lower layers may realize comparable elements in higher layers; e.g., a

---

[1] Note that this was called "used by" in previous versions of the standard. For the sake of clarity, this name has been changed to "serving".

"data object" (Application Layer) may realize a "business object" (Business Layer); or an "artifact" (Technology Layer) may realize either a "data object" or an "application component" (Application Layer).

3.4 The ArchiMate Core Framework

The ArchiMate Core Framework is a framework of nine cells used to classify elements of the ArchiMate core language. It is made up of three aspects and three layers, as illustrated in Figure 2. This is known as the ArchiMate Core Framework.

It is important to understand that the classification of elements based on aspects and layers is only a global one. Real-life architecture elements need not strictly be confined to one aspect or layer because elements that link the different aspects and layers, play a central role in a coherent architectural description. For example, running somewhat ahead of the later conceptual discussions, business roles serve as intermediary elements between "purely behavioral" elements and "purely structural" elements, and it may depend on the context whether a certain piece of software is considered to be part of the Application Layer or the Technology Layer.

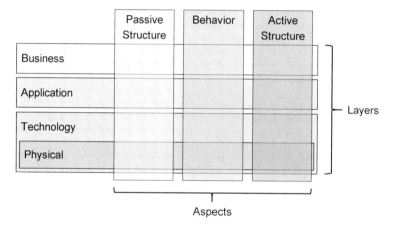

Figure 2: ArchiMate Core Framework

The structure of the framework allows for modeling of the enterprise from different viewpoints, where the position within the cells highlights the concerns of the stakeholder. A stakeholder typically can have concerns that cover multiple cells.

The dimensions of the framework are as follows:

- Layers – the three levels at which an enterprise can be modeled in ArchiMate – Business, Application, and Technology (as described in Section 3.3)

- Aspects:

  — The *Active Structure Aspect*, which represents the structural elements (the business actors, application components, and devices that display actual behavior; i.e., the "subjects" of activity)

The Open Group Standard (2022)

— The *Behavior Aspect*, which represents the behavior (processes, functions, events, and services) performed by the actors; structural elements are assigned to behavioral elements, to show who or what displays the behavior

— The *Passive Structure Aspect*, which represents the objects on which behavior is performed; these are usually information objects in the Business Layer and data objects in the Application Layer, but they may also be used to represent physical objects

These three aspects were inspired by natural language where a sentence has a subject (active structure), a verb (behavior), and an object (passive structure). By using the same constructs that people are used to in their own languages, the ArchiMate language is easier to learn and read.

Since ArchiMate notation is a *graphical* language where elements are organized spatially, this order is of no consequence in modeling.

A composite element, as shown in Figure 1, is an element that does not necessarily fit in a single aspect (column) of the framework but may combine two or more aspects.

Note that the ArchiMate language does not require the modeler to use any particular layout such as the structure of this framework; it is merely a categorization of the language elements.

3.5   The ArchiMate Full Framework

The ArchiMate Full Framework, as described in this version of the standard, adds a number of layers and an aspect to the Core Framework. The physical elements are included in the Technology Layer for modeling physical facilities and equipment, distribution networks, and materials. As such, these are also core elements. The strategy elements are introduced to model strategic direction and choices. They are described in Chapter 7. The motivation aspect is introduced at a generic level in the next chapter and described in detail in Chapter 6. The implementation and migration elements are described in Chapter 12. The resulting ArchiMate Full Framework is shown in Figure 3.

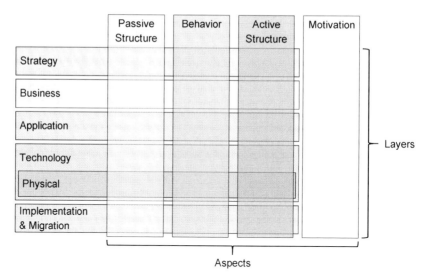

Figure 3: ArchiMate Full Framework

The ArchiMate language does not define a specific layer for information; however, elements from the passive structure aspect such as business objects, data objects, and artifacts are used to represent information entities. Information modeling is supported across the different ArchiMate layers.

3.6 Abstraction in the ArchiMate Language

The structure of the ArchiMate language accommodates several familiar forms of abstraction and refinement. First of all, the distinction between an external (black-box, abstracting from the contents of the box) and internal (white-box) view is common in systems design. The external view depicts what the system has to do for its environment, while the internal view depicts how it does this.

Second, the distinction between behavior and active structure is commonly used to separate what the system must do and how the system does it from the system constituents (people, applications, and infrastructure) that do it. In modeling new systems, it is often useful to start with the behaviors that the system must perform, while in modeling existing systems, it is often useful to start with the people, applications, and infrastructure that comprise the system, and then analyze in detail the behaviors performed by these active structures.

A third distinction is between conceptual, logical, and physical abstraction levels. This has its roots in data modeling: conceptual elements represent the information the business finds relevant; logical elements provide logical structure to this information for manipulation by information systems; physical elements describe the storage of this information; for example, in the form of files or database tables. In the ArchiMate language, this corresponds with business objects, data objects, and artifacts, along with the realization relationships between them.

The distinction between logical and physical elements has also been carried over to the description of applications. The TOGAF Enterprise Metamodel [4] includes a set of entities that describe business, data, application, and technology components and services to describe architecture concepts. Logical components are implementation or product-independent encapsulations of data or functionality, whereas physical components are tangible software components, devices, etc. This distinction is captured in the TOGAF framework in the form of Architecture Building Blocks (ABBs) and Solution Building Blocks (SBBs). This distinction is again useful in progressing Enterprise Architectures from high-level, abstract descriptions to tangible, implementation-level designs. Note that building blocks may contain multiple elements, which are typically modeled using the grouping concept in the ArchiMate language.

The ArchiMate language has three ways of modeling such abstractions. First, as described in [6], behavior elements such as application and technology functions can be used to model logical components, since they represent implementation-independent encapsulations of functionality. The corresponding physical components can then be modeled using active structure elements such as application components and nodes, assigned to the behavior elements. Second, the ArchiMate language supports the concept of realization. This can best be described by working with the Technology Layer upwards. The Technology Layer defines the physical artifacts and software that realize an application component. It also provides a mapping to other physical concepts such as devices, networks, etc. needed for the realization of an information system. The realization relationship is also used to model more abstract kinds of realization, such as that between a (more specific) requirement and a (more generic) principle, where fulfillment of the requirement implies adherence to the principle. Realization is also allowed between application components and between nodes. This way you can model a physical application or technology component realizing a logical application or technology component, respectively. Third, logical and physical application components can be defined as metamodel-level specializations of the application component element, as described in Chapter 14 (see also the examples in Section 14.2.2). The same holds for the logical and physical technology components of the TOGAF Content Metamodel, which can be defined as specializations of the node element (see Section 14.2.3).

The ArchiMate language intentionally does not support a difference between types and instances. At the Enterprise Architecture abstraction level, it is more common to model types and/or exemplars rather than instances. Similarly, a business process in the ArchiMate language does not describe an individual instance (i.e., one execution of that process). In most cases, a business object is therefore used to model an object type (*cf.* a UML® class), of which several instances may exist within the organization. For instance, each execution of an insurance application process may result in a specific instance of the insurance policy business object, but that is not modeled in the Enterprise Architecture.

3.7 Concepts and their Notation

The ArchiMate language separates the language concepts (i.e., the constituents of the metamodel) from their notation. Different stakeholder groups may require different notations in order to understand an architecture model or view. In this respect, the ArchiMate language differs from languages such as UML or BPMN™, which have only one standardized notation. The viewpoint mechanism explained in Chapter 13 provides the means for defining such stakeholder-oriented visualizations.

Although the notation of the ArchiMate concepts can (and should) be stakeholder-specific, the standard provides one common graphical notation which can be used by architects and others who develop ArchiMate models. This notation is targeted towards an audience used to existing technical modeling techniques such as Entity Relationship Diagrams (ERDs), UML, or BPMN, and therefore resembles them. In the remainder of this document, unless otherwise noted, the symbols used to depict the language concepts represent the ArchiMate standard notation. This standard notation for most elements consists of a box with an icon in the upper-right corner. In several cases, this icon by itself may also be used as an alternative notation. This standard iconography should be preferred whenever possible so that anyone knowing the ArchiMate language can read the diagrams produced in the language.

3.8 Use of Nesting

Nesting elements inside other elements can be used as an alternative graphical notation to express some relationships. This is explained in more detail in Chapter 5 and in the definition of each of these relationships.

3.9 Use of Colors and Notational Cues

In the metamodel pictures within this standard, shades of grey are used to distinguish elements belonging to the different aspects of the ArchiMate framework, as follows:

- White for abstract (i.e., non-instantiable) concepts
- Light grey for passive structures
- Medium grey for behavior
- Dark grey for active structures

In ArchiMate models, there are no formal semantics assigned to colors and the use of color is left to the modeler. However, they can be used freely to stress certain aspects in models. For instance, in many of the example models presented in this standard, colors are used to distinguish between the layers of the ArchiMate Core Framework, as follows:

- Yellow for the Business Layer
- Blue for the Application Layer
- Green for the Technology Layer

They can also be used for visual emphasis. A recommended text providing guidelines is Chapter 6 of [1]. In addition to the colors, other notational cues can be used to distinguish between the layers of the framework. A letter M, S, B, A, T, P, or I in the top-left corner of an element can be used to denote a Motivation, Strategy, Business, Application, Technology, Physical, or Implementation & Migration element, respectively. An example of this notation is depicted in Example 34.

The standard notation also uses a convention with the shape of the corners of its symbols for different element types, as follows:

- Square corners are used to denote structure elements
- Round corners are used to denote behavior elements
- Diagonal corners are used to denote motivation elements

4 Generic Metamodel

Note: The relationships shown in the metamodel figures are not to be confused with ArchiMate relationships. They are metamodel relationships expressing the structure of the language rather than a model *in* the language.

4.1 Behavior and Structure Elements

The main hierarchy of behavior and structure elements of the ArchiMate language is presented in the metamodel fragment of Figure 4. It defines these elements in a generic, layer-independent way. Note that most of these elements (the white boxes) are *abstract* metamodel elements; i.e., these are not instantiated in models but only serve to structure the metamodel. The notation presented in this chapter is therefore the generic way in which the specializations of these elements (i.e., the elements of the different architecture layers) are depicted.

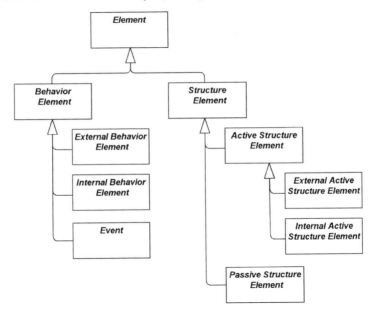

Figure 4: Hierarchy of Behavior and Structure Elements

This generic metamodel fragment consists of two main types of elements: *structure* ("nouns") and *behavior* elements ("verbs").

Structure elements can be subdivided into *active structure* elements and *passive structure* elements. Active structure elements can be further subdivided into *external* active structure elements (also called *interfaces*) and *internal* active structure elements.

Behavior elements can be subdivided into *internal behavior* elements, *external behavior* elements (also called *services*), and *events*.

Figure 5 specifies the main relationships between the behavior and structure elements defined above. For an explanation of the different types of relationships see Chapter 5. In this and other metamodel figures, the label of a relationship signifies the role of the source element in the relationship; e.g., a service serves an internal behavior element.

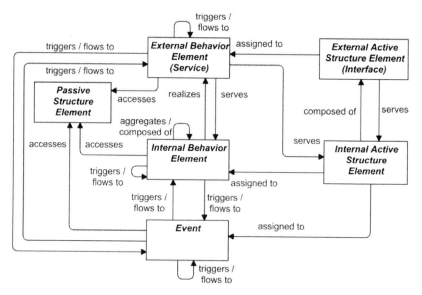

Figure 5: Behavior and Structure Elements Metamodel

Note: This figure does not show all permitted relationships; every element in the language can have composition, aggregation, and specialization relationships to elements of the same type. Furthermore, there are indirect relationships that can be derived, as explained in Section 5.7. The full specification of permitted relationships can be found in Appendix B.

Note: This figure is to be read as a generic template for the layers of the ArchiMate core (see Section 3.4), but is not applied directly. Each layer defines its own specialized version of this.

4.1.1   Active Structure Elements

Active structure elements are the subjects that can perform behavior. These can be subdivided into internal active structure elements; i.e., the business actors, application components, nodes, etc., that realize this behavior, and external active structure elements; i.e., the interfaces that expose this behavior to the environment. An interface provides an external view on the service provider and hides its internal structure.

An internal active structure element represents an entity that is capable of performing behavior.

Active structure elements are denoted using boxes with square corners and an icon in the upper-right corner, or by the icon on its own.

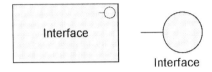

Figure 6: Generic Internal Active Structure Element Notation

An external active structure element, called an interface, represents a point of access where one or more services are provided to the environment.

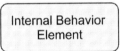

Figure 7: Generic External Active Structure Elements (Interface) Notation

4.1.2 Behavior Elements

Behavior elements represent the dynamic aspects of the enterprise. Similar to active structure elements, behavior elements can be subdivided into *internal* behavior elements and *external* behavior elements; i.e., the services that are exposed to the environment.

An internal behavior element represents a unit of activity that can be performed by one or more active structure elements.

Behavior elements are denoted in the standard iconography using boxes with round corners and an icon in the upper-right corner, or by the icon on its own.

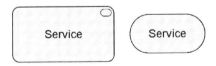

Figure 8: Generic Internal Behavior Element Notation

An external behavior element, called a service, represents an explicitly defined exposed behavior.

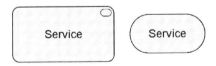

Figure 9: Generic External Behavior Element (Service) Notation

Thus, a service is the externally visible behavior of the providing system, from the perspective of systems that use that service; the environment consists of everything outside this providing system. The value offered to the user of the service provides the motivation for the existence of the service. For the users, only this exposed behavior and value, together with non-functional aspects such as the quality of service, costs, etc., are relevant. These can be specified in a contract or Service-Level Agreement (SLA). Services are accessible through interfaces.

In addition to this, a third type of behavior element is defined to denote an event that can occur; for example, to signal a state change.

> An event represents a state change.

An event may have a time attribute that indicates the moment or moments at which the event happens. For example, this can be used to model time schedules.

Figure 10: Generic Event Notation

4.1.3 Passive Structure Elements

Passive structure elements can be accessed by behavior elements.

> A passive structure element represents an element on which behavior is performed.

A passive structure element is a structural element that cannot perform behavior. Active structure elements can perform behavior on passive structure elements. Passive structure elements are often information or data objects, but they can also represent physical objects.

Figure 11: Generic Passive Structure Element Notation

4.2 Specializations of Structure and Behavior Elements

The specializations of core elements are summarized in Figure 12. Within each layer, it is permitted to use composition and aggregation relationships between processes, functions, and interactions; e.g., a process can be composed of other processes, functions, and/or interactions.

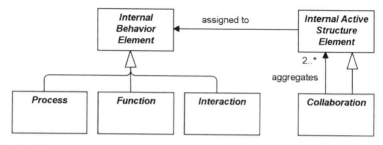

Figure 12: Specializations of Core Elements

For individual internal behavior elements, a distinction is made between processes and functions.

A process represents a sequence of behaviors that achieves a specific result.

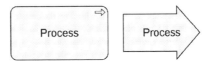

Figure 13: Generic Process Notation

A function represents a collection of behavior based on specific criteria, such as required resources, competencies, or location, and is managed, performed, or implemented as a whole.

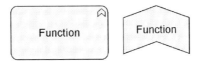

Figure 14: Generic Function Notation

Internal behavior elements can be composed of or aggregate other internal behavior elements, as shown in Figure 5. This means, for instance, that processes can be composed of functions and *vice versa*.

The collective nature of a behavior can be modeled either implicitly (several active structure elements assigned to the same internal behavior via an *and* junction) or explicitly through the use of a collective internal behavior element, interaction, that is performed by (a collaboration of) multiple active structure elements.

An interaction represents a unit of collective behavior that must be performed by two or more internal active structure elements, either assigned directly or aggregated in a collaboration.

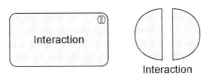

Figure 15: Generic Interaction Notation

A collaboration represents an aggregate of two or more internal active structure elements, working together to perform some collective behavior.

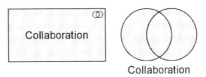

Figure 16: Generic Collaboration Notation

4.3   Summary of Structure and Behavior Elements

Table 1 gives an overview of the core elements, their definitions, and their default graphical notation. But note that most of these elements are abstract; they are not used in models but only their descendants in the different layers of the ArchiMate language.

Table 1: Core Elements

Element	Specializations	Definition	Notation
Active Structure			
Internal Active Structure Element		Represents an entity that is capable of performing behavior.	Internal Active Structure Element
	Collaboration	Represents an aggregate of two or more internal active structure elements, working together to perform some collective behavior.	Collaboration / Collaboration
Interface (External Active Structure Element)		Represents a point of access where one or more services are exposed to the environment.	Interface / Interface
Behavior			
Internal Behavior Element		Represents a unit of activity that can be performed by one or more active structure elements.	Internal Behavior Element
	Process	Represents a sequence of behaviors that achieves a specific result.	Process / Process
	Function	Represents a collection of behavior based on specific criteria, such as required resources, competencies, or location, and is managed, performed, or implemented as a whole.	Function / Function
	Interaction	Represents a unit of collective behavior that must be performed by two or more internal active structure elements, either assigned directly or aggregated in a collaboration.	Interaction / Interaction
Service (External Behavior Element)		Represents an explicitly defined exposed behavior.	Service / Service
Event		Represents a state change.	Event / Event

Element	Specializations	Definition	Notation	
Passive Structure				
Passive Structure Element		Represents an element on which behavior is performed.	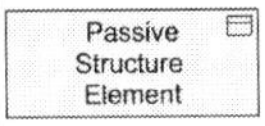 Passive Structure Element 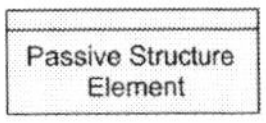 ⊟	Passive Structure Element

4.4   Motivation Elements

The core elements of the ArchiMate language focus on describing the architecture of systems that support the enterprise. They do not cover the elements which, in different ways, *drive* the design and operation of the enterprise. These motivation aspects correspond to the "Why" column of the Zachman framework [5].

Several *motivation elements* are included in the language: stakeholder, value, meaning, driver, assessment, goal, outcome, principle, and requirement, which in turn has constraint as a subtype. In this section, the generic motivation element is introduced. The more specific motivation elements are described in Chapter 6.

The motivation elements address the way the Enterprise Architecture is aligned to its context, as described by these intentions.

A motivation element represents the context of or reason behind the architecture of an enterprise.

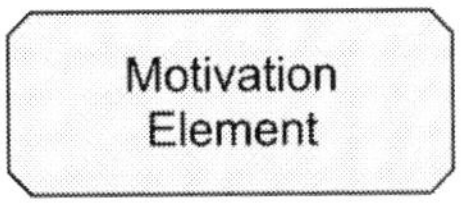

Figure 17: Generic Motivation Element Notation

Motivation elements are usually denoted using boxes with diagonal corners.

Table 2: Motivation Element

Element	Definition	Notation
Motivation Element	Represents the context of or reason behind the architecture of an enterprise.	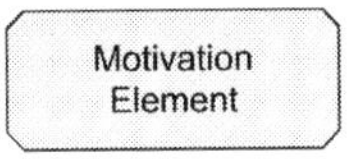 Motivation Element

4.5   Composite Elements

Composite elements consist of other concepts, possibly from multiple aspects or layers of the language. Grouping and location are generic composite elements (see Figure 18). Other composite elements include Product (see Section 8.5.1) and Plateau (see Section 12.2.4). Composite elements can themselves aggregate or compose other composite elements.

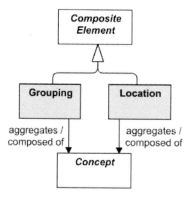

Figure 18: Composite Elements

4.5.1   Grouping

> The grouping element aggregates or composes concepts that belong together based on some common characteristic.

The grouping element is used to aggregate or compose an arbitrary group of concepts, which can be elements and/or relationships of the same or of different types. An aggregation or composition relationship is used to link the grouping element to the grouped concepts. Grouping elements can also have other relationships to and from them, as shown in Appendix B.

Figure 19: Grouping Notation

Concepts may be aggregated by multiple (overlapping) groups.

One useful way of employing grouping is for modeling Architecture and Solution Building Blocks (ABBs and SBBs), as described in the TOGAF framework [4].

Another useful application of grouping is for modeling domains. For example, the TOGAF framework [4] Glossary of Supplementary Definition defines Information Domain as: *"grouping of information (or data entities) by a set of criteria such as security classification, ownership, location, etc. In the context of security, Information Domains are defined as a set of users, their information objects, and a security policy"*.

Note: The use of grouping is not to be confused with creating views on the architecture (Section 13.3). Although like a view it comprises concepts that belong together for some reason, it does not provide a separate visualization of these concepts. Moreover, groupings are used *within* architecture views to provide additional structure to an architecture model and its visualization.

Example

In Example 1, the "Grouping" element is used to aggregate a conglomerate of two processes and an object that together realize a service (both with nesting and explicitly drawn aggregation relationships).

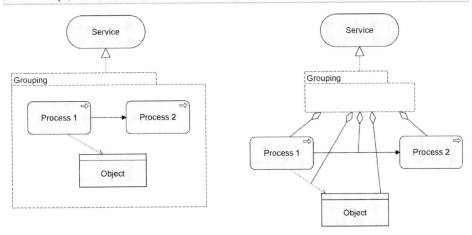

Example 1: Grouping

Note: The semantics of grouping imply that a relationship from or to a group should be interpreted as a collective relationship with the group's contents. In the example, the implied meaning is that the contents of the group together, or parts thereof, realize the service. However, this is not always easily expressed in simple derivable relationships.

4.5.2   Location

A location represents a conceptual or physical place or position where concepts are located (e.g., structure elements) or performed (e.g., behavior elements).

The location element is used to model the places where (active and passive) structure elements such as business actors, application components, and devices are located. This is modeled by means of an aggregation relationship from a location to structure element. A location can also aggregate a behavior element, to indicate where the behavior is performed. This element corresponds to the "Where" column of the Zachman framework [5].

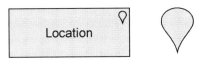

Figure 20: Location Notation

5 Relationships and Relationship Connectors

In addition to the generic elements outlined in Chapter 4, the ArchiMate language defines a core set of generic relationships, each of which can connect a predefined set of source and target concepts (in most cases elements, but in a few cases also other relationships). Many of these relationships are "overloaded"; i.e., their exact meaning differs depending on the source and destination concepts that they connect.

The relationships are classified as follows (see Figure 21):

- *Structural* relationships, which model the static construction or composition of concepts of the same or different types

- *Dependency* relationships, which model how elements are used to support other elements

- *Dynamic* relationships, which are used to model behavioral dependencies between elements

- *Other* relationships, which do not fall into one of the above categories

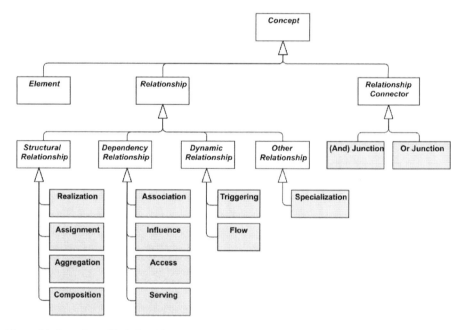

Figure 21: Overview of Relationships

Each relationship has exactly one "from" and one "to" concept (element, relationship, or relationship connector) as endpoints. The following restrictions apply:

- No relationships are allowed between two relationships

- All relationships connected with relationship connectors must be of the same type

- A chain of relationships of the same type that connects two elements, and is in turn connected via relationship connectors, is valid only if a direct relationship of that same type between those two elements is valid

- A relationship connecting an element with a second relationship can only be an aggregation, composition, or association; aggregation or composition are valid only from a composite element to that second relationship

It is good practice to explicitly name or label any relationship that would else be ambiguous or otherwise misunderstood.

For the sake of readability, the metamodel figures throughout this document do not show all possible relationships in the language. Section 5.7 describes a set of derivation rules to derive indirect relationships between elements in a model. Aggregation, composition, and specialization relationships are always permitted between two elements of the same type, and association is always allowed between any two elements, and between any element and relationship. The exact specification of permitted relationships is given in Appendix B.

5.1 Structural Relationships

Structural relationships represent the "static" coherence within an architecture. The uniting (composing, aggregating, assigned, or realizing) concept (the "from" side of the relationship) is always an element; for assignment and realization it can be an element or a relationships connector. The united (being composed, aggregated, assigned to, or realized) concept (the "to" side of the relationship) may in some cases also be another relationship or relationship connector.

As an alternative to the graphical notations proposed in this section, structural relationships may also be expressed by nesting the united concept within the uniting element. Note, however, that this can lead to ambiguous views (although unambiguous in the model), in case multiple structural relationships are allowed between these elements.

5.1.1 Composition Relationship

The composition relationship represents that an element consists of one or more other concepts.

The composition relationship has been inspired by the composition relationship in UML class diagrams. Composition is a whole/part relationship that expresses an existence dependency: if a composite is deleted, its parts are (normally) deleted as well. When you model real-world elements – for example, an organization structure of departments and teams expressed as business actors – this dependency applies to these elements themselves. When you model exemplars or categories – as is common in Enterprise Architecture – this dependency may be interpreted as applying to their real-world instances. For example, a specific kind of server can be modeled as a node composed of a device and system software; this implies an existence dependency between individual servers of that kind and the individual devices and system software instances of which they consist.

A composition relationship is always allowed between two instances of the same element type.

In addition to this, the metamodel explicitly defines other source and target elements that may be connected by a composition relationship.

Figure 22: Composition Notation

The interpretation of a composition relationship is that the *whole or part* of the source element is composed of the *whole of* the target element. See also Section 5.1.5.

Example

Example 2 shows the two ways to express that the "Financial Processing" business function is composed of three sub-functions.

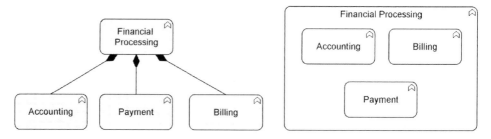

Example 2: Composition

5.1.2 Aggregation Relationship

The aggregation relationship represents that an element combines one or more other concepts.

The aggregation relationship has been inspired by the aggregation relationship in UML class diagrams. Unlike composition, aggregation does not imply an existence dependency between the aggregating and aggregated concepts.

An aggregation relationship is always allowed between two instances of the same element type.

In addition to this, the metamodel explicitly defines other source and target elements that may be connected by an aggregation relationship.

Figure 23: Aggregation Notation

The interpretation of an aggregation relationship is that the *whole or part* of the source element aggregates the *whole of* the target concept. See also Section 5.1.5.

Example

Example 3 shows two ways to express that the "Customer File" aggregates an "Insurance Policy" and "Insurance Claim".

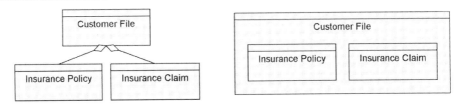

Example 3: Aggregation

5.1.3   Assignment Relationship

The assignment relationship represents the allocation of responsibility, performance of behavior, storage, or execution.

The assignment relationship links active structure elements with units of behavior that are performed by them, business actors with business roles that are fulfilled by them, and nodes with technology passive structure elements. It can, for example, relate an internal active structure element with an internal behavior element, an interface with a service, or a node, device, and system software with an artifact. The full set of permitted relationships is listed in Appendix B.

Figure 24: Assignment Notation

In the ArchiMate framework described in Section 3.4, it always points from active structure to behavior, from behavior to passive structure, and from active to passive structure. The non-directional notation from the ArchiMate 2.1 Specification and before, which shows the black ball at both ends of the relationship, is still allowed but deprecated.

As with all structural relationships, an assignment relationship can also be expressed by nesting the model elements. The direction mentioned above is also the direction of nesting; for example, a business role inside the business actor performing that role, an application function inside an application component executing that function, or an artifact inside a node that stores it.

The interpretation of an assignment relationship is that the *whole or part* of the source element is assigned the *whole of* the target element (see also Section 5.1.5). This means that if, for example, two active structure elements are assigned to the same behavior element, either of them can perform the complete behavior. If both active structure elements are needed to perform the behavior, the grouping element or a junction (see Section 5.5) can be used, and if the combination of these elements has a more substantive and independent character, a collaboration would be the right way to express this.

Example

Example 4 includes the two ways to express the assignment relationship. The "Finance" application component is assigned to the "Transaction Processing" application function, and the "Payment Interface" is assigned to the "Payment Service".

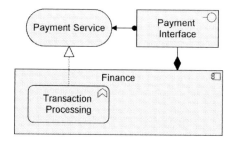

Example 4: Assignment

5.1.4   Realization Relationship

The realization relationship represents that an element plays a critical role in the creation, achievement, sustenance, or operation of a more abstract element.

The realization relationship indicates that more abstract elements ("what" or "logical") are realized by means of more tangible elements ("how" or "physical"). The realization relationship is used to model run-time realization; for example, that a business process realizes a business service, and that a data object realizes a business object, an artifact realizes an application component, or a core element realizes a motivation element.

Figure 25: Realization Notation

The interpretation of a realization relationship is that the *whole or part* of the source element realizes the *whole of* the target element (see also Section 5.1.5). This means that if, for example, two internal behavior elements have a realization relationship to the same service, either of them can realize the complete service. If both internal behavior elements are needed to realize, the grouping element or an *and* junction (see Section 5.5.1) can be used. For weaker types of effects on the realization of a motivation element, the influence relationship (see Section 5.2.3) should be used.

Example

Example 5 illustrates two ways to use the realization relationship. A "Transaction Processing" business function realizes a "Billing Service"; the "Billing Data" business object is realized by the representation "Paper Invoice".

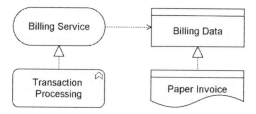

Example 5: Realization

5.1.5 Semantics of Structural Relationships

Structural relationships describe that the element on the source side contains, groups, performs, or realizes the concept on the target side of the relationship. Structural relationships can be transitively applied to (possibly unmodeled) parts of the source element. Below are some examples of how these semantics work:

- Composition and aggregation relationships from parts also apply to the whole

  For example, if a part of A aggregates B, A itself is also considered to aggregate B. Conversely, if A aggregates B, that can be interpreted as some part of A aggregating B.

- Assignment relationships to behavior elements also apply to the active structure elements

  For example, if business role A is assigned to business process B, some part of A may perform B. Conversely, if a part of A is assigned to B, A itself is also considered to be assigned to B.

- Realization relationships to external behavior elements also apply to the internal behavior elements

  For example, if a service B is realized by a process A, B may be realized by some part of A. Conversely, if a part of A realizes B, A itself is also considered to realize B.

Example

In the left-hand side of Example 6, the entire business actor B (possibly a department) is composed in business actor A (possibly a division), via some unmodeled element inside A. In the example on the right, business process A completely realizes business service B, via some unmodeled element inside A.

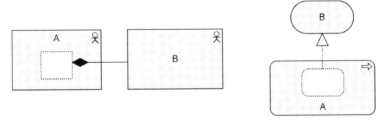

Example 6: Semantics of Structural Relationships

5.2 Dependency Relationships

Dependency relationships describe how elements support or are used by other elements. Four types of dependency relationship are distinguished:

- The *serving* relationship represents a *control* dependency, denoted by a solid line
- The *access* relationship represents a *data* dependency, denoted by a dotted line
- The *influence* relationship represents an *impact* dependency, denoted by a dashed line

- The *association* relationship represents a dependency not covered by any of the other relationships

Note that, although the notation of these relationships resembles the notation of the dependency relationship in UML, these relationships have distinct meanings in ArchiMate notation and (usually) point in the opposite direction. One advantage of this is that it yields models with directionality, where most of the arrows that represent such supporting, influencing, serving, or realizing dependencies point "upwards" towards the client/user/business, as you can see in the layered viewpoint example in Section C.1.5. Another reason for this direction, in particular for the serving relationship, is that it abstracts from the "caller" or "initiator", since a service may be delivered proactively or reactively. The direction of delivery is always the same, but the starting point for the interaction can be on either end. UML's dependency is often used to denote the latter, showing that the caller depends on some operation that is called. However, for modeling this type of initiative, the ArchiMate language provides the triggering relationship (Section 5.3.1), which can be interpreted as a dynamic (i.e., temporal) dependency. Similarly, the flow relationship is used to model how something (usually information) is transferred from one element to another, which is also a dynamic kind of dependency.

5.2.1 Serving Relationship

The serving relationship represents that an element provides its functionality to another element.

The serving relationship describes how the services or interfaces offered by a behavior or active structure element serve entities in their environment. This relationship is applied for both the behavior aspect and the active structure aspect.

Compared to the earlier versions of this standard, the name of this relationship has been changed from "used by" to "serving", to better reflect its direction with an active verb: a service serves a user. The meaning of the relationship has not been altered. The "used by" designation is still allowed but deprecated, and will be removed in a future version of the standard.

$$\longrightarrow$$

Figure 26: Serving Notation

Example

Example 7 illustrates the serving relationship. The "Payment Interface" serves the "Customer", while the "Payment Service" serves the "Pay Invoices" business process of that customer.

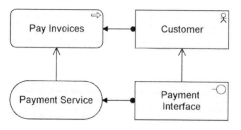

Example 7: Serving

5.2.2 Access Relationship

> The access relationship represents the ability of behavior and active structure elements to observe or act upon passive structure elements.

The access relationship indicates that a process, function, interaction, service, or event "does something" with a passive structure element; e.g., create a new object, read data from the object, write or modify the object data, or delete the object. The relationship can also be used to indicate that the object is just associated with the behavior; e.g., it models the information that comes with an event, or the information that is made available as part of a service. The arrowhead, if present, indicates the creation, change, or usage of passive structure elements. The access relationship should not be confused with the UML dependency relationship, which uses a similar notation.

Note that, at the metamodel level, the direction of the relationship is always from an active structure element or a behavior element to a passive structure element, although the notation may point in the other direction to denote "read" access, and in both directions to denote read-write access. Care must be taken when using access with derived relationships because the arrow on the relationship has no bearing to its directionality.

Figure 27: Access Notation

Alternatively, an access relationship can be expressed by nesting the passive structure element inside the behavior or active structure element that accesses it; for example, nesting a data object inside an application component.

Example

> Example 8 illustrates the access relationship. The "Create Invoice" sub-process writes/creates the "Invoice" business object; the "Send Invoice" sub-process reads that object.

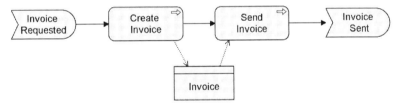

Example 8: Access

5.2.3 Influence Relationship

> The influence relationship represents that an element affects the implementation or achievement of some motivation element.

The influence relationship is used to describe some architectural elements that influence the achievement or implementation of a motivation element, such as a goal or a principle. In general, a motivation element is realized to a certain degree. For example, consistently satisfying the principle "serve customers wherever they are", will help to make the goal "increase market share", come true. In other words, the principle contributes to the goal. In turn, to implement the principle "serve customers wherever they are", it may be useful to impose a requirement of "24x7 web availability" on some customer-facing application component. This can be modeled as a requirement that has an influence on that principle and as an application component that in turn influences the requirement. Consistently modeling these dependencies with an influence relationship yields a traceable motivational path that explains why, in this example, a certain application component contributes to the corporate goal to "increase market share". This kind of traceability supports measuring the results of Enterprise Architecture and provides valuable information to, for example, change impact assessments.

Additional to this "vertical" use of contribution, from core elements upwards to requirements and goals, the relationship can also be used to model "horizontal" contributions between motivation elements. The influence relationship in that case describes that some motivation element may influence (the achievement or implementation of) another motivation element. In general, a motivation element is achieved to a certain degree. An influence by some other element may affect this depending on the degree in which the other element is satisfied itself. For example, the degree in which a goal to increase customer satisfaction is realized, may be represented by the percentage of satisfied customers that participate in a market interview. This percentage may be influenced by, for example, the goal to improve the reputation of the company; i.e., a higher degree of improvement results in a higher increase in customer satisfaction. On the other hand, the goal to lay off employees may influence the company reputation negatively; i.e., more lay-offs could result in a lower increase (or even decrease) in the company reputation. Thus (indirectly), the goal to increase customer satisfaction may also be influenced negatively.

The realization relationship should be used to represent relationships that are critical to the existence or realization of the target. The influence relationship should be used to represent relationships that are not critical to the target object's existence or realization. For example, a business actor representing a construction crew may realize the goal of constructing a building, and a requirement to add additional skilled \ workers to an already adequate crew may influence the goal of constructing the building. However, the business actor also realizes an additional goal of opening the building by a particular date. An influence relationship can be used to model either:

- The fact that an element positively contributes to the achievement or implementation of some motivation element, or

- The fact that an element negatively influences – i.e., prevents or counteracts – such achievement

Attributes can be used to indicate the sign and/or strength of the influence. The choice of possible attribute values is left to the modeler; e.g., {++, +, 0, -, --} or [0..10]. By default, the influence relationship models a contribution with unspecified sign and strength.

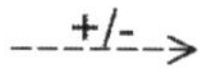

$$--\underline{+/-}-\!\!\gg$$

Figure 28: Influence Notation

Example

Example 9 illustrates the use of the influence relationship to model the different effects of the same requirement, "Assign Personal Assistant". This has a strongly positive influence on "Reduce Workload Of Employees", but a strongly negative influence on "Decrease Costs".

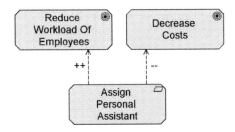

Example 9: Influence

5.2.4   Association Relationship

An association relationship represents an unspecified relationship, or one that is not represented by another ArchiMate relationship.

An association relationship is always allowed between two elements, or between a relationship and an element.

The association relationship can be used when drawing a first high-level model where relationships are initially denoted in a generic way, and later refined to show more specific relationship types. In the metamodel pictures, some specific uses of the association relationship are explicitly shown. An association is undirected by default but may be directed. See also Section 5.2.5.

Figure 29: Association Notation

Example

Example 10 illustrates two directed association relationships between a contract and two business objects to which this contract refers. It also shows an association between a flow relationship and this contract, to indicate that the contract is transferred from Policy Creation to Policy Management.

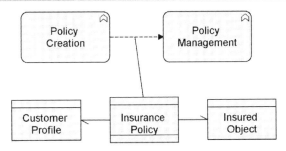

Example 10: Association

5.2.5   Semantics of Dependency Relationships

Dependency relationships describe that a part of the target element has a dependency on a part of the source element. Although there is a dependency between the two elements, it does not necessarily mean this applies to all of the parts of the element as defined by any structural relationships.

This semantic allows you to model dependencies at a high level (with details removed) without implying specific dependencies at a more detailed level. This means, for example, that:

- In serving relationships, some part of an internal behavior element is served by some part of an external behavior element; for example, if a business service A serves a business process B, some unmodeled sub-service of A may serve an unmodeled sub-process of B

- In access relationships, some part of a behavior element accesses some part of a passive structure element; for example, if an application function A accesses a data object B, some unmodeled sub-function of A may access an unmodeled part of B

- In influence relationships, some part of a core element influences some part of a motivational element; for example, if an application component A influences a requirement B, some unmodeled part of A may influence some unmodeled part of B

- In association relationships, some part of an element is related to some part of another element; if it is directed, it can only be used in derivations in that direction (see Section 5.7)

Example

In the left-hand side of Example 11, a part of business process B is served by a part of application service A. In the right-hand example, a part of business process B accesses (reads) a part of business object A.

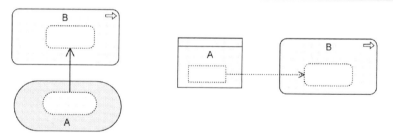

Example 11: Semantics of Dependency Relationships

5.3   Dynamic Relationships

The dynamic relationships describe temporal dependencies between elements within the architecture. Two types of dynamic relationships are distinguished: *triggering* and *flow*.

5.3.1   Triggering Relationship

The triggering relationship represents a temporal or causal relationship between elements.

The triggering relationship is used to model the temporal or causal precedence of behavior elements in a process. The interpretation of a triggering relationship is that some part of the source element should be completed before the target element can start (see also Section 5.3.3). Note that this does not necessarily represent that one behavior element actively starts another; a traffic light turning green also triggers the cars to go through the intersection.

Figure 30: Triggering Notation

Example

Example 12 illustrates that triggering relationships are used to model causal dependencies between (sub-)processes and/or events.

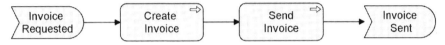

Example 12: Triggering

5.3.2   Flow Relationship

The flow relationship represents transfer from one element to another.

The flow relationship is used to model the flow of, for example, information, goods, or money between behavior elements. A flow relationship does not imply a causal relationship.

Figure 31: Flow Notation

Example

Example 13 shows a "Claim Assessment" business function, which forwards decisions about the claims to the "Claim Settlement" business function. In order to determine the order in which the claims should be assessed, "Claim Assessment" makes use of schedule information received from the "Scheduling" business function.

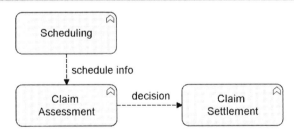

Example 13: Flow

5.3.3 Semantics of Dynamic Relationships

The semantics of triggering and flow relationships differ. The triggering relationship follows the same semantics as structural relationships (Section 5.1.5). A triggering relationship from A to B indicates that everything in B is preceded by a part of A. When A and B are business processes, for example, it means that all steps in business process B are performed after a part of A has occurred, but steps in A can occur after some or all steps in B have occurred. A stronger interpretation of triggering (everything in B is preceded by everything in A) could be imposed on the ArchiMate model by a modeling group wishing to do so.

The flow relationships follow the same semantics as dependency relationships (see Section 5.2.5). A flow relationship from A to B indicates that the whole or some part of A transfers something (e.g., information) to the whole or some part of B.

5.4 Other Relationships

5.4.1 Specialization Relationship

The specialization relationship represents that an element is a particular kind of another element.

The specialization relationship has been inspired by the generalization relationship in UML class diagrams but is applicable to specialize a wider range of concepts.

A specialization relationship is always allowed between two instances of the same element type.

Figure 32: Specialization Notation

Alternatively, a specialization relationship can be expressed by nesting the specialized element inside the generic element.

Example

Example 14 illustrates the use of the specialization relationship for a process. In this case, the "Take Out Travel Insurance" and "Take Out Luggage Insurance" business processes are a specialization of a more generic "Take Out Insurance" business process.

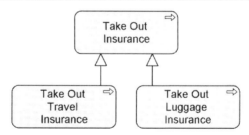

Example 14: Specialization

5.4.2 Semantics of Other Relationships

The semantics of the specialization relationship are that the whole of the generic element is specialized by the specialized element.

5.5 Relationship Connectors

5.5.1 Junction

A junction is not an actual relationship in the same sense as the other relationships described in this chapter, but rather a relationship connector.

> A junction is used to connect relationships of the same type.

A path with junctions that connect relationships of a specific type is only allowed between two concepts if a direct relationship of that type between these concepts is also permitted. Simply put, you cannot use junctions to create relationships between concepts that would otherwise not be allowed.

A junction may have multiple incoming relationships and one outgoing relationship, one incoming relationship and multiple outgoing relationships, or multiple incoming and outgoing relationships (the latter can be considered a shorthand of two contiguous junctions).

A junction is used to explicitly express that all elements together must participate in the relationship (*and* junction) or that at least one of the elements participates in the relationship (*or* junction). The *or* junction can be used to express both inclusive and exclusive or conditions, which could be indicated by a modeler by naming the junction to reflect its type.

In addition to the above, a junction (which connects some relationships), may also be aggregated or composed in a plateau, grouping, or location element. If that junction connects other aggregation or composition relationships, it should be interpreted without the aggregation or composition to this containing element. The composition or aggregation merely states that the junction is part of a plateau, grouping, or location. Without that relationship, the junction must fulfill the same conditions as above: it connects relationships of the same type, with at least one incoming and one outgoing relationship.

It is allowed to omit arrowheads of relationships leading into a junction.

(And) Junction   Or Junction

Figure 33: Junction Notation

Junctions may be used on triggering relationships. This is a technique used by other modeling languages. For example, the BPMN notation uses gateways as junctions, and the UML notation uses forks and joins in their modeling activity diagrams. They can be used to model high-level process flow. A label may be added to outgoing triggering relationships of a junction to indicate a choice, condition, or guard that applies to that relationship. Such a label is only an informal indication. No formal, operational semantics have been defined for these relationships because implementation-level languages such as BPMN and UML, differ in their execution semantics and the ArchiMate language does not want to unduly constrain mappings to such languages.

Examples

In Example 15, the *and* junction in the model is used to denote that the "Sales" and "Finance" business functions together realize the "Invoicing" business service.

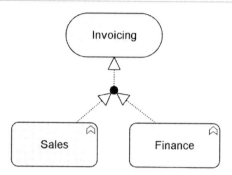

Example 15: (And) Junction

In Example 16, the *or* junction is used to denote a choice: business process "Assess Request" triggers either "Accept Request" or "Reject Request". (The usual interpretation of two separate triggering relations, one from "Assess Request" to "Accept Request" and one from "Assess Request" to "Reject Request", is that "Assess Request" triggers both of the other business processes.)

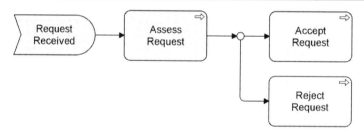

Example 16: Or Junction

5.6   Summary of Relationships

Table 3 gives an overview of the ArchiMate relationships with their definitions.

Table 3: Relationships

Structural Relationships		Notation	Role Names
Composition	Represents that an element consists of one or more other concepts.	◆—	→ composed of ← composed in
Aggregation	Represents that an element combines one or more other concepts.	◇—	→ aggregates ← aggregated in

Assignment	Represents the allocation of responsibility, performance of behavior, storage, or execution.	●——————▶	→ assigned to ← has assigned
Realization	Represents that an element plays a critical role in the creation, achievement, sustenance, or operation of a more abstract element.	·········▷	→ realizes ← realized by
Dependency Relationships		**Notation**	**Role Names**
Serving	Represents that an element provides its functionality to another element.	———————▷	→ serves ← served by
Access	Represents the ability of behavior and active structure elements to observe or act upon passive structure elements.	················ ················▷ ◁················▷	→ accesses ← accessed by
Influence	Represents that an element affects the implementation or achievement of some motivation element.	__±/__▷	→ influences ← influenced by
Association	Represents an unspecified relationship, or one that is not represented by another ArchiMate relationship.	———————— ————————▷	associated with → associated to ← associated from
Dynamic Relationships		**Notation**	**Role Names**
Triggering	Represents a temporal or causal relationship between elements.	——————▶	→ triggers ← triggered by
Flow	Represents transfer from one element to another.	------▶	→ flows to ← flows from
Other Relationships		**Notation**	**Role Names**
Specialization	Represents that an element is a particular kind of another element.	———————▷	→ specializes ← specialized by
Relationship Connectors		**Notation**	**Role Names**
Junction	Used to connect relationships of the same type.	● (And) Junction ○ Or Junction	

5.7 Derivation of Relationships

In the ArchiMate language, you can derive indirect relationships between elements in a model, based on the modeled relationships. This makes it possible to abstract from intermediary elements that are not relevant in order to show a certain model or view of the architecture that supports impact analysis. The precise rules for making such derivations are specified in Appendix B.

Example

In Example 17, assume that the goal is to abstract from the application functions, sub-functions, and services in the model. In this case, an indirect serving relationship (thick red arrow on the right) can be derived from "Financial Application" to the "Invoicing and Collections" business process (from the chain assignment – composition – realization – serving).

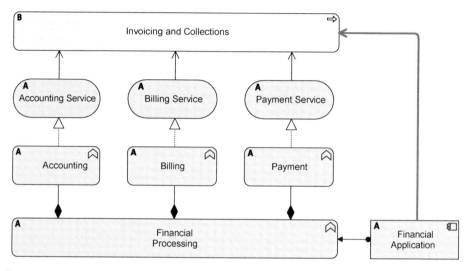

Example 17: Derivation from a Chain of Relationships

Derivation of relationships is intended as a way to create summaries of detailed models. It is a way to remove (to abstract from) details in a model while still making valid "statements". Hence, derivation is always meant to go from more detail to less detail. This mechanism is one of the unique properties of the ArchiMate language compared to other modeling languages.

The language allows the modeler to directly create relationships that are necessarily valid derived relationships without the constituents of the derivation being available in the model. These relationships (for example, a realization relationship between an application component and an application service) assume that the required constituents (for example, an application function) needed for the derived relationship exist; however, these missing elements need not be modeled explicitly, and the derived relationships can be used as if they have not been derived. Thus, the modeler has full freedom in choosing the required level of detail.

Because the essence of derivation is to make simplifications or summaries, it cannot be used to infer more detail. For example, a realization relationship from an application component to an application service can be modeled, but from it no conclusions can be drawn about the exact source of this derivation (e.g., which functions realize which services).

This is information that should be added by a modeler during the design process: a higher-level, more abstract model can be refined by elaborating the derived relationships (in the previous example by adding an application function that realizes the application service and to which the application component is assigned).

It is important to note that all these derived relationships are also valid in the ArchiMate language. They are not shown in the metamodel diagrams included in the standard because this would reduce their legibility. However, the tables in Appendix B show all permitted relationships between two elements in the language.

6 Motivation Elements

Motivation elements are used to model the motivations, or reasons, that guide the design or change of an Enterprise Architecture.

6.1 Motivation Elements Metamodel

Figure 34 gives an overview of the motivation elements and their relationships.

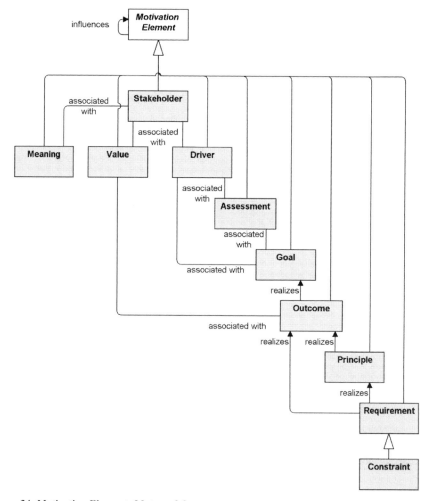

Figure 34: Motivation Elements Metamodel

Note: This figure does not show all permitted relationships; every element in the language can have composition, aggregation, and specialization relationships with elements of the same type. Furthermore, there are indirect relationships that can be derived, as explained in Section 5.7. The full specification of permitted relationships can be found in Appendix B.

6.2 Stakeholder, Driver, and Assessment

It is essential to understand the factors, often referred to as *drivers*, which influence other motivation elements. They can originate from either inside or outside the enterprise. A *stakeholder* can be an individual or a group of people, such as a project team, enterprise, or society. Drivers that are associated with a stakeholder are often called "concerns" of that stakeholder. Examples of such drivers are customer satisfaction, compliance to legislation, or profitability. It is common for enterprises to undertake an *assessment* of these drivers; e.g., using a Strengths, Weaknesses, Opportunities, and Threats (SWOT) analysis, in order to respond in the best way.

6.2.1 Stakeholder

A stakeholder represents the role of an individual, team, or organization (or classes thereof) that represents their interests in the effects of the architecture.

This definition is based on the definition in the TOGAF framework [4]. A stakeholder has one or more interests in, or concerns about, the organization and its Enterprise Architecture. In order to direct efforts to these interests and concerns, stakeholders change, set, and emphasize goals. Stakeholders may also influence each other. Examples of stakeholders are the Chief Executive Officer (CEO), the board of directors, shareholders, customers, business and application architects, but also legislative authorities. The name of a stakeholder should preferably be a noun.

Figure 35: Stakeholder Notation

6.2.2 Driver

A driver represents an external or internal condition that motivates an organization to define its goals and implement the changes necessary to achieve them.

Drivers that are associated with a stakeholder are often called "concerns" of that stakeholder. Stakeholder concerns are defined in the TOGAF framework [4] as "*an interest in a system relevant to one or more of its stakeholders. Concerns may pertain to any aspect of the system's functioning, development, or operation, including considerations such as performance, reliability, security, distribution, and evolvability and may determine the acceptability of the system.*" Examples of internal drivers are customer satisfaction and profitability. Drivers of change may also be external to the enterprise (e.g., economic changes or changing legislation) and need not have a stakeholder associated with them. The name of a driver should preferably be a noun.

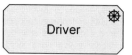

Figure 36: Driver Notation

6.2.3   Assessment

> An assessment represents the result of an analysis of the state of affairs of the enterprise with respect to some driver.

An assessment may reveal strengths, weaknesses, opportunities, or threats for some area of interest. These need to be addressed by adjusting existing goals or setting new ones, which may trigger changes to the Enterprise Architecture.

Strengths and weaknesses are internal to the organization. Opportunities and threats are external to the organization. Weaknesses and threats can be considered as problems that need to be addressed by goals that "negate" the weaknesses and threats. Strengths and opportunities may be translated directly into goals. For example, the weakness "Customers complain about the helpdesk" can be addressed by defining the goal "Improve helpdesk". Or the opportunity "Customers favor insurances that can be managed online" can be addressed by the goal "Introduce online portfolio management". The name of an assessment should preferably be a noun or a (very) short sentence.

Figure 37: Assessment Notation

6.2.4   Example

> The stakeholder "Chief Marketing Officer (CMO)" is concerned with the driver "Market Share", the stakeholder "Chief Executive Officer (CEO)" is concerned with the drivers "Market Share" and "Profitability", and the stakeholder "Chief Financial Officer (CFO)" is concerned with the driver "Profitability". The driver "Profitability" is composed of two other drivers: "Revenue" and "Costs". Several assessments are associated with these drivers (e.g., the assessment "Market Share Is Declining" is associated with driver "Market Share"), and assessments may influence each other in a positive or negative way (e.g., "Market Share Is Declining" results in "Revenue Is Declining", which in turn results in "Profitability Is Declining").

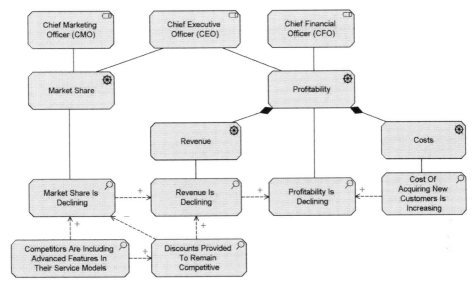

Example 18: Stakeholder, Driver, and Assessment

6.3 Goal, Outcome, Principle, Requirement, and Constraint

The motivation of an organization or individual to achieve certain results is represented by goals, principles, requirements, and constraints. *Goals* represent that a stakeholder wants to realize a certain outcome; e.g., "Increase customer satisfaction by 10%". The end results realized by capabilities that realize these goals are *outcomes*. Principles and requirements represent desired properties of solutions – or means – to realize the goals. *Principles* are normative guidelines that guide the design of all possible solutions in a given context. For example, the principle "Data should be stored only once" represents a means to achieve the goal of "Data consistency" and applies to all possible designs of the organization's architecture. *Requirements* represent formal statements of need, expressed by stakeholders, which must be met by the architecture or solutions. For example, the requirement "Use a single CRM system" conforms to the aforementioned principle by applying it to the current organization's architecture in the context of the management of customer data.

6.3.1 Goal

A goal represents a high-level statement of intent, direction, or desired end state for an organization and its stakeholders.

In principle, a goal can represent anything a stakeholder may desire, such as a state of affairs, or a produced value. Examples of goals are: to increase profit, to reduce waiting times at the helpdesk, or to introduce online portfolio management. Goals are typically used to measure success of an organization.

Goals are generally expressed using qualitative words; e.g., "increase", "improve", or "easier". Goals can also be decomposed; e.g., "increase profit" can be decomposed into the goals "reduce cost" and "increase sales". However, it is also very common to associate concrete outcomes with goals, which can be used to describe both the quantitative and time-related results that are essential to describe the desired state, and when it should be achieved.

Figure 38: Goal Notation

6.3.2 Outcome

An outcome represents an end result, effect, or consequence of a certain state of affairs.

Outcomes are high-level, business-oriented results produced by capabilities of an organization, and by inference by the core elements of its architecture that realize these capabilities. Outcomes are tangible, possibly quantitative, and time-related, and can be associated with assessments. An outcome may have a different value for different stakeholders.

The notion of outcome is important in business outcome-driven approaches to Enterprise Architecture and in capability-based planning. Outcomes are closely related to requirements, goals, and other intentions. The distinction between goals and outcomes is important. Simply put, a goal is what you want, and an outcome is what you get. Outcomes are the end results, and goals or requirements are often related to outcomes that should be realized. Capabilities can be designed to achieve such outcomes.

However, not all outcomes relate to goals. When modeling a future state, an outcome models some result or effect that is expected to have been achieved or occur at that future point in time. Unlike goals, outcomes can also be used to model potentially unwanted effects; for example, in order to design appropriate mitigating measures.

Outcome names should unambiguously identify end results that have been achieved or are expected to be achieved at a definite point in the future. Examples include "First-place customer satisfaction ranking achieved" and "Key supplier partnerships in place". Outcome names can also be more specific; e.g., "10% year-over-year quarterly profits increase in 2018".

Figure 39: Outcome Notation

6.3.3 Principle

A principle represents a statement of intent defining a general property that applies to any system in a certain context in the architecture.

The term "system" is used in its general meaning; i.e., as a group of (functionally) related elements, where each element may be considered as a system again. Therefore, a system may refer to any active structural element, behavior element, or passive structural element of some organization, such as a business actor, application component, business process, application service, business object, or data object.

Principles are strongly related to goals and requirements. Similar to requirements, principles define intended properties of systems. However, in contrast to requirements, principles are broader in scope and more abstract than requirements. A principle defines a general property that applies to any system in a certain context, whereas a requirement defines a property that applies to a specific system as described by an architecture. For example, the principle "Information management processes comply with all relevant laws, policies, and regulations" is realized by the requirements that are imposed by the actual laws, policies, and regulations that apply to the specific system under design.

Figure 40: Principle Notation

6.3.4 Requirement

A requirement represents a statement of need defining a property that applies to a specific system as described by the architecture.

In the end, a business goal must be realized by a plan or concrete change goal, which may or may not require a new system or changes to an existing system.

Requirements model the properties of these elements that are needed to achieve the "ends" that are modeled by the goals. In this respect, requirements represent the "means" to realize goals.

During the design process, goals may be decomposed until the resulting sub-goals are sufficiently detailed to enable their realization by properties that can be exhibited by systems. At this point, goals can be realized by requirements that demand these properties from the systems.

For example, two alternative requirements may be identified to realize the goal "Improve portfolio management":

- By assigning a personal assistant to each customer, or
- By introducing online portfolio management

The former requirement can be realized by a human actor and the latter by a software application. These requirements can be decomposed further to define the requirements on the human actor and the software application in more detail.

Figure 41: Requirement Notation

6.3.5 Constraint

A constraint represents a limitation on aspects of the architecture, its implementation process, or its realization.

In contrast to a requirement, a constraint does not prescribe some intended functionality of the system to be realized but imposes a restriction on the way it operates or may be realized. This may be a restriction on the implementation of the system (e.g., specific technology that is to be used), a restriction on the implementation process (e.g., time or budget constraints), or a restriction on the functioning of the system (e.g., legal constraints).

Figure 42: Constraint Notation

6.3.6 Example

The goal "Improve Profitability of Service Offering" is realized by the outcome "Increased Profit by 10% in Next Fiscal Year". This outcome is influenced positively by the outcomes "Increased Revenue by 20% in Next Fiscal Year" and "Reduced Cost of Customer Acquisition by 25%". The outcome "Increased Revenue by 20% in Next Fiscal Year" is influenced positively by an outcome "Increased Market Share by 10% in Next Fiscal Year". There is also a negative outcome: "Increased Technology Expenditure by 10%". These outcomes are realized by a combination of two principles: "Serve Customers Wherever They Are" and "Serve Customers Whenever They Need Our Help". Both of these principles are realized by a combination of two requirements: "Mobile Applications Shall Run On All Popular Mobile Platforms" and "Services Shall Be Accessible Through Mobile Browsers". The outcome "Reduced Cost Of Customer Acquisition by 25%" is realized by a principle "Respond To Changing Customer Needs, Preferences, And Expectations Quickly And Efficiently", which in turn is realized by a constraint "Mobile Applications Shall Be Built With Cross-Platform Frameworks".

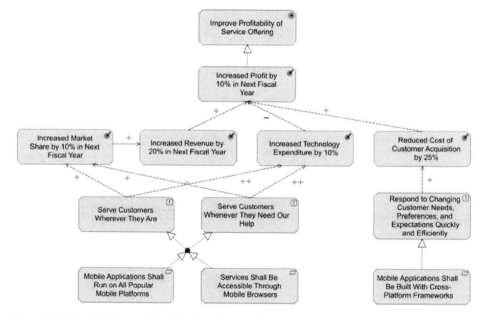

Example 19: Goal, Outcome, Principle, Requirement, and Constraint

6.4 Meaning and Value

Different stakeholders may attach a different *value* to outcomes since they may have different interests. Similarly, they may give their own *meaning* or interpretation to core elements of the architecture.

6.4.1 Meaning

> Meaning represents the knowledge or expertise present in, or the interpretation given to, a concept in a particular context.

A meaning represents the interpretation of a concept of the architecture. In particular, this is used to describe the meaning of passive structure elements (for example, a document, message). It is a description that expresses the *intent* of that element; i.e., how it informs the *external user*.

It is possible that different users view the informative functionality of an element differently. For example, what may be a "registration confirmation" for a client could be a "client mutation" for a CRM department (assuming for the sake of argument that it is modeled as an external user). Also, various different representations may carry essentially the same meaning. For example, various different documents (a web document, a filled-in paper form, a "client contact" report from the call center) may essentially carry the same meaning.

A meaning can be associated with any concept. To denote that a meaning is specific to a particular stakeholder, this stakeholder can also be associated to the meaning. The name of a meaning should preferably be a noun or noun phrase.

Figure 43: Meaning Notation

6.4.2 Value

> Value represents the relative worth, utility, or importance of a concept.

Value represents the usefulness, advantage, benefit, desirability, or gain for a customer, stakeholder, or end user by, for example, selling a product, using a service, or completing some activity. Value is often expressed in terms of money, but it has long since been recognized that non-monetary value is also essential to business; for example, practical/functional value (including the *right* to use a service), and the value of information or knowledge. Though value can hold internally for some system or organizational unit, it is most typically applied to *external* appreciation of goods, services, information, knowledge, or money, normally as part of some sort of customer-provider relationship.

A value can be associated with any concept. To model the stakeholder for whom this value applies, this stakeholder can also be associated with that value. Although the name of a value can be expressed in many different ways (including amounts, objects), where the "functional" value of an architecture element is concerned, it is recommended to try and express it as an action or state that can be performed or reached as a result of the corresponding element being available.

Figure 44: Value Notation

6.4.3　Example

Sending push notifications has a value of "Cost Efficiency" for the stakeholder "Insurer", and a value of "Being Informed" and "Peace of Mind" (which is partly due to a value of "Certainty") for the stakeholder "Customer". Different meanings can be assigned to the different specific types of notification messages. A "Confirmation Of Receipt Message" has the meaning "Claim Has Been Received", a "Review Complete Message" has the meaning "Claim Review Complete", and a "Payment Complete Message" has the meaning "Claim Has Been Paid".

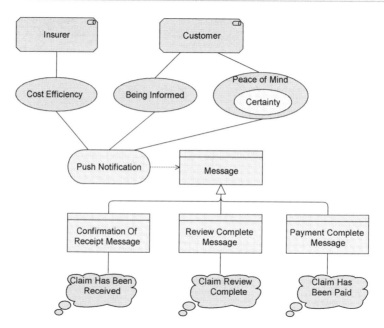

Example 20: Meaning and Value

6.5   Summary of Motivation Elements

Table 4 gives an overview of the motivation elements, with their definitions.

Table 4: Motivation Elements

Element	Definition	Notation
Stakeholder	Represents the role of an individual, team, or organization (or classes thereof) that represents their interests in the effects of the architecture.	Stakeholder
Driver	Represents an external or internal condition that motivates an organization to define its goals and implement the changes necessary to achieve them.	Driver
Assessment	Represents the result of an analysis of the state of affairs of the enterprise with respect to some driver.	Assessment
Goal	Represents a high-level statement of intent, direction, or desired end state for an organization and its stakeholders.	Goal
Outcome	Represents an end result, effect, or consequence of a certain state of affairs.	Outcome
Principle	Represents a statement of intent defining a general property that applies to any system in a certain context in the architecture.	Principle
Requirement	Represents a statement of need defining a property that applies to a specific system as described by the architecture.	Requirement
Constraint	Represents a limitation on aspects of the architecture, its implementation process, or its realization.	Constraint
Meaning	Represents the knowledge or expertise present in, or the interpretation given to, a concept in a particular context.	Meaning
Value	Represents the relative worth, utility, or importance of a concept.	Value

6.6   Relationships with Core Elements

The purpose of the motivation elements is to model the motivation behind the core elements in an Enterprise Architecture. Therefore, it should be possible to relate motivation elements to core elements.

As shown in Figure 45, a requirement (and, indirectly, also a principle, outcome, and goal) can be related directly to a structure or behavior element by means of a realization relationship. Also, the weaker influence relationship is allowed between these elements. Meaning and value can be associated with any structure or behavior element.

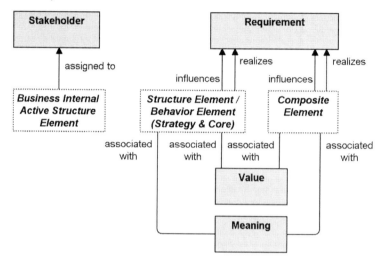

Figure 45: Relationships Between Motivation Elements and Core Elements

Additionally, a business internal active structure element (i.e., business actor, role, or collaboration) may be assigned to a stakeholder to express that someone with an operational position within the enterprise is also a stakeholder of that enterprise.

7 Strategy Layer

The strategy elements are typically used to model the strategic direction and choices of an enterprise, as far as the impact on its architecture is concerned. They can be used to express how the enterprise wants to create value for its stakeholders, the capabilities it needs, the resources needed to support these capabilities, as well as how it plans to configure and use these capabilities and resources to achieve its aims (see Chapter 6). Strategy elements are used to model the strategic direction and choices of the enterprise, whereas Business Layer elements (Chapter 8) are used to model the operational organization of an enterprise.

Intentionally, the set of elements in the Strategy Layer is kept as small and simple as possible. The Strategy elements are more abstract than the Business elements. The Strategy Layer abstracts from the difference between active and passive structure, and from the internal/external distinction in the Business, Application, and Technology layers. Unlike these layers, it therefore does not have service or interface elements.

7.1 Strategy Elements Metamodel

Figure 46 gives an overview of the strategy elements and their relationships. Note that "Course of Action" is a behavior element but not a strategy behavior element, because it models a different type of behavior and has a different set of relationships.

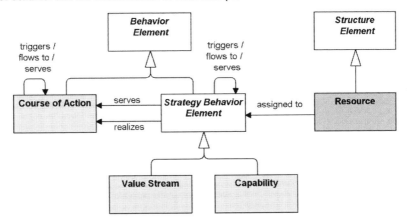

Figure 46: Strategy Elements Metamodel

Note: This figure does not show all permitted relationships; every element in the language can have composition, aggregation, and specialization relationships with elements of the same type. Furthermore, there are indirect relationships that can be derived, as explained in Section 5.7. The full specification of permitted relationships can be found in Appendix B.

7.2   Structure Elements

7.2.1   Resource

> A resource represents an asset owned or controlled by an individual or organization.

Resources are a central concept in the field of strategic management, economics, computer science, portfolio management, and more. They are often recognized along with capabilities, to be sources of competitive advantage for organizations. Resources are analyzed in terms of strengths and weaknesses, and considered when implementing strategies. Due to resources being limited, they can often be a deciding factor for choosing which strategy, goal, and project to implement and in which order. Resources can be classified in different ways; including tangible assets, intangible assets, and human assets. Examples of tangible assets include financial assets (cash, securities, borrowing capacity, etc.) and physical assets (plant, equipment, land, mineral reserves, etc.). Examples of intangible assets include technology assets (patents, copyrights, trade secrets, etc.), reputation assets (brand, relationships, etc.), and culture assets. Examples of human assets include skills/know-how, capacity for communication and collaboration, and motivation.

Resources are realized by active and passive structure elements and are therefore classified as structures that are neither active nor passive. The name of a resource should preferably be a noun.

Figure 47: Resource Notation

7.3   Behavior Elements

7.3.1   Capability

> A capability represents an ability that an active structure element, such as an organization, person, or system, possesses.

In the field of business, strategic thinking and planning delivers strategies and high-level goals that are often not directly implementable in the architecture of an organization. These long-term or generic plans need to be specified and made actionable in a way that both business leaders and Enterprise Architects can relate to, and at a relatively high abstraction level.

Capabilities help to reduce this gap by focusing on business outcomes. On the one hand, they provide a high-level view of the current and desired abilities of an organization, in relation to its strategy and its environment. On the other hand, they are realized by various elements (people, processes, systems, and so on) that can be described, designed, and implemented using Enterprise Architecture approaches. Capabilities may also have serving relationships; for example, to denote that one capability contributes to another.

Capabilities are classified as behavior in the ArchiMate language because they describe abilities: what the enterprise can (is able to) *do* (now or in the future). Capabilities are expressed in general, high-level terms that are typically realized by a combination of organization, people, processes, information, and technology. For example, business planning, customer management, or asset management [21]. This capability concept corresponds to the business capability in the TOGAF framework [6].

Capabilities are typically aimed at achieving some goal. Capabilities are themselves realized by core elements. To denote that a set of core elements together realizes a capability, grouping can be used.

Capabilities are often used for capability-based planning, to describe their evolution over time. To model such so-called capability increments, the specialization relationship can be used to denote that a certain capability increment is a specific version of that capability. Aggregating those increments and the core elements that realize them in plateaus (see Section 12.2.4) can be used to model the evolution of the capabilities.

The name of a capability should emphasize "what we do" rather than "how we do it". Typically, it should be expressed as a compound noun or gerund (-ing form of verb); e.g., "Risk Management", "Market Development", "Product Engineering", etc.

Figure 48: Capability Notation

7.3.2   Value Stream

A value stream represents a sequence of activities that create an overall result for a customer, stakeholder, or end user.

A value stream describes how an enterprise organizes its activities to create value. As described in the TOGAF Series Guide: Value Streams [17], a key principle of value streams is that value is always defined from the perspective of the stakeholder – the customer, end user, or recipient of the product, service, or deliverable produced by the work. The value obtained is in the eye of the beholder; it depends more on the stakeholder's perception of the worth of the product, service, outcome, or deliverable than on its intrinsic value; i.e., the cost to produce. This is modeled in the ArchiMate language by using the value element and in turn, is associated on the one hand with the result being produced, and on the other hand may be associated with the stakeholder.

Value streams may be defined at different levels of the organization; e.g., at the enterprise level, business unit level, or department level. Value streams can be a composition or aggregation of value-adding activities. These are also modeled with the value stream element and known as value (stream) stages. Each of which creates and adds incremental value from one stage to the next. These stages are typically related using flow relationships to model the flow of value between them. Resources can be assigned to value streams and capabilities can serve (i.e., enable) a value stream.

Importantly, value streams and business processes may seem alike, but they are defined at different abstraction levels and serve separate purposes. A business process describes the (time-ordered) sequence of behaviors required to create some result for an individual case, and it may describe alternative paths and decision points (modeled with junctions). In contrast, a value stream focuses on the overall value-creating behavior from the perspective of the importance, worth, or usefulness of what is produced, and is not a description of time-ordered tasks for individual cases. Value streams (and capabilities) reflect an organization's business model and value proposition, whereas business processes (and business functions) reflect its operating model. At their respective abstraction levels, value streams and business processes both represent the "enterprise in motion", whereas capabilities and business functions both describe the "enterprise at rest".

Value streams are typically realized by business processes and possibly other core behavior elements. The stages in a value stream provide a framework for organizing and defining business processes, but different parts of the organization may have their own implementations of business processes that realize the same value stream stage.

It is recommended that the name of a value stream be expressed using a verb-noun construct in the active tense; e.g., "Acquire Insurance Product".

Figure 49: Value Stream Notation

7.3.3 Course of Action

> A course of action represents an approach or plan for configuring some capabilities and resources of the enterprise, undertaken to achieve a goal.

A course of action represents what an enterprise has decided to do. Courses of action can be categorized as strategies and tactics. It is not possible to make a hard distinction between the two, but strategies tend to be long-term and fairly broad in scope, while tactics tend to be shorter-term and narrower in scope.

Figure 50: Course of Action Notation

7.4 Example

> "Increase Profit" is a goal that can be decomposed into a number of other goals: "Decrease Costs" and "Increase Revenue". The former is related to the "Operational Excellence" strategy of the company, modeled as a course of action. This is decomposed into two other courses of action: "Centralize IT Systems" and "Standardize Products". These result in two outcomes: "Decreased Costs" and "Loss of Customers", which influence the goals in positive and negative ways. This shows an important difference between goals and outcomes: not all outcomes lead to the intended results.
>
> The courses of action are realized by a number of capabilities: "IT Management & Operations" and "Product Management", and appropriate resources "Human Resources" and "IT Resources" are assigned to the former. The model fragment also shows that these resources are located in the "Headquarters" of the organization, in line with the "Centralize IT Systems" course of action.

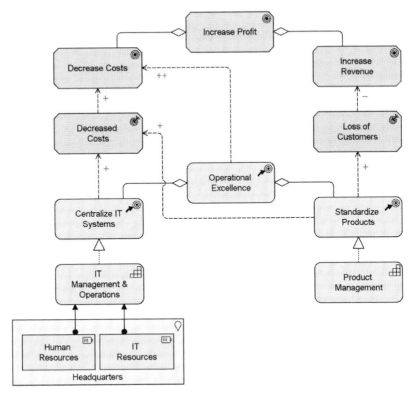

Example 21: Capability, Resource, and Course of Action

Example 22 shows a model of a high-level value stream for an insurance company, where each stage in the value stream is served by a number of capabilities. Between these stages, we see the value flows with associated value items, and at the end the business outcome that this value stream realizes for a particular stakeholder.

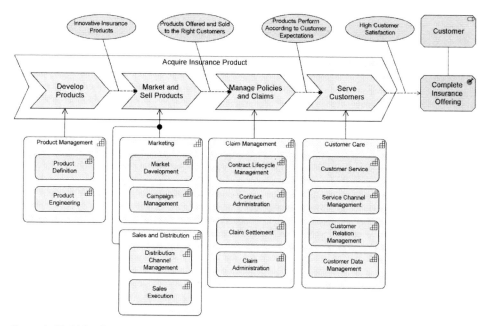

Example 22: Value Stream with Capability Cross-Mapping

7.5   Summary of Strategy Elements

Table 5 gives an overview of the strategy elements, with their definitions.

Table 5: Strategy Elements

Element	Description	Notation	
Resource	Represents an asset owned or controlled by an individual or organization.	Resource	
Capability	Represents an ability that an active structure element, such as an organization, person, or system, possesses.	Capability	
Value Stream	Represents a sequence of activities that create an overall result for a customer, stakeholder, or end user.	Value Stream	
Course of Action	Represents an approach or plan for configuring some capabilities and resources of the enterprise, undertaken to achieve a goal.	Course of Action	

7.6 Relationships with Motivation and Core Elements

Figure 51 shows how the strategy elements are related to core elements and motivation elements. Internal and external behavior elements may realize strategy behavior elements (value streams and capabilities), while an active or passive structure element may realize a resource. Capabilities, value streams, courses of action, and resources may realize or influence requirements (and indirectly, as described in Section 5.7, also principles or goals), and a course of action may also realize or influence an outcome (and, indirectly, also a goal).

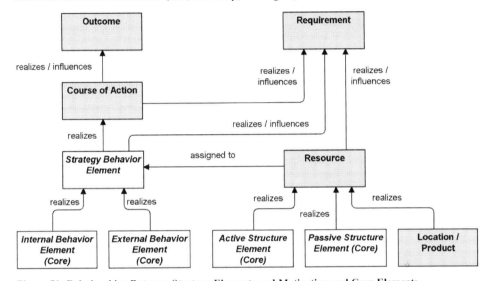

Figure 51: Relationships Between Strategy Elements and Motivation and Core Elements

8 Business Layer

Business Layer elements are used to model the operational organization of an enterprise in a technology-independent manner, whereas strategy elements (Chapter 7) are used to model the strategic direction and choices of the enterprise.

8.1 Business Layer Metamodel

Figure 52 gives an overview of the Business Layer elements and their relationships. "Business Internal Active Structure Element", "Business Internal Behavior Element", and "Business Passive Structure Element" are abstract elements; only their specializations (as defined in the following sections) are instantiated in models.

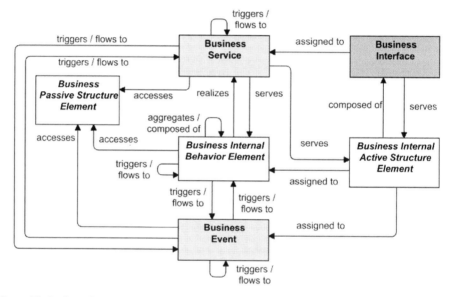

Figure 52: Business Layer Metamodel

Note: This figure does not show all permitted relationships; every element in the language can have composition, aggregation, and specialization relationships with elements of the same type. Furthermore, there are indirect relationships that can be derived, as explained in Section 5.7.

8.2 Active Structure Elements

The active structure aspect of the Business Layer refers to the static structure of an organization, in terms of the entities that make up the organization and their relationships. The *active entities* are the subjects (e.g., business actors or business roles) that perform behavior such as business processes or functions (capabilities). Business actors may be individual persons (e.g., customers or employees), but also groups of people (organization units) and resources that have a permanent (or at least long-term) status within the organizations. Typical examples of the latter are a department and a business unit.

Architectural descriptions focus on structure, which means that the inter-relationships of entities within an organization play an important role. To make this explicit, the element of business collaboration has been introduced.

The element of business interface is introduced to explicitly model the (logical or physical) places or channels where the services that a role offers to the environment can be accessed. The same service may be offered on a number of different interfaces; e.g., by mail, by telephone, or through the Internet. In contrast to application modeling, it is uncommon in current Business Layer modeling approaches to recognize the business interface element.

In the Business Layer, three types of internal active structure element are defined: *business actor*, *business role*, and *business collaboration*.

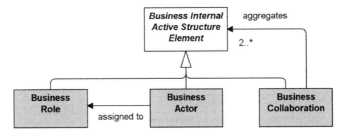

Figure 53: Business Internal Active Structure Elements

Note: This figure does not show all permitted relationships; every element in the language can have composition, aggregation, and specialization relationships with elements of the same type. Furthermore, there are indirect relationships that can be derived, as explained in Section 5.7. The full specification of permitted relationships can be found in Appendix B.

8.2.1   Business Actor

A business actor represents a business entity that is capable of performing behavior.

A business actor is a business entity as opposed to a technical entity; i.e., it belongs to the Business Layer. Actors may, however, include entities outside the actual organization; e.g., customers and partners. A business actor can represent such business entities at different levels of detail and may correspond to both an actor and an organizational unit in the TOGAF framework [4]. Examples of business actors are humans, departments, and business units.

A business actor may be assigned to one or more business roles. It can then perform the behavior to which these business roles are assigned. A business actor can be aggregated in a location. The name of a business actor should preferably be a noun. Business actors may be specific individuals or organizations; e.g., "John Smith" or "ABC Corporation", or they may be generic; e.g., "customer" or "supplier".

Figure 54: Business Actor Notation

8.2.2 Business Role

> A business role represents the responsibility for performing specific behavior, to which an actor can be assigned, or the part an actor plays in a particular action or event.

Business roles with certain responsibilities or skills are assigned to business processes or business functions. A business actor that is assigned to a business role is responsible for ensuring that the corresponding behavior is carried out, either by performing it or by delegating and managing its performance. In addition to the relation of a business role with behavior, a business role is also useful in a (structural) organizational sense; for instance, in the division of labor within an organization.

A business role may be assigned to one or more business processes or business functions, while a business actor may be assigned to one or more business roles. A business interface or an application interface may serve a business role, while a business interface may be part of a business role. The name of a business role should preferably be a noun.

Figure 55: Business Role Notation

ArchiMate modelers may represent generic organizational entities that perform behavior as either business actors or business roles. For example, the business actor "Supplier" depicts an organizational entity, while the business role "Supplier" depicts a responsibility. Specific or generic business actors can be assigned to carry responsibilities depicted as business roles. For example, the specific business actor "ABC Corporation" or the generic business actor "Business Partner" can be assigned to the "Supplier" business role.

8.2.3 Business Collaboration

> A business collaboration represents an aggregate of two or more business internal active structure elements that work together to perform collective behavior.

A business process or function may be interpreted as the internal behavior of a single business internal active structure element. In some cases, behavior is the collective effort of more than one business internal active structure element; in fact, a collaboration of two or more business internal active structure elements results in collective behavior which may be more than simply the sum of the behavior of the separate elements. Business collaborations represent this collective effort. Business interactions can be used to describe the internal behavior that takes place within business collaboration. A business collaboration is a (possibly temporary) collection of business roles, actors, or other collaborations within an organization which perform collaborative behavior (interactions). Unlike a department, a business collaboration need not have an official (permanent) status within the organization; it is specifically aimed at a specific interaction or set of interactions between roles. It is especially useful in modeling Business-to-Business (B2B) interactions between different organizations such as provider networks, and also for describing social networks.

A business collaboration may aggregate a number of business roles, actors, or other collaborations and may be assigned to one or more business interactions or other business internal behavior elements. A business interface or an application interface may serve a business collaboration, while a business collaboration may have business interfaces (through composition, and also through aggregation via derived relationships). The name of a business collaboration should preferably be a noun. It is also rather common to leave a business collaboration unnamed.

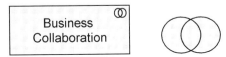

Figure 56: Business Collaboration Notation

8.2.4   Business Interface

A business interface represents a point of access where business services are made available to the environment.

A business interface exposes the functionality of a business service to other business roles or actors. It is often referred to as a channel (telephone, Internet, local office, etc.). The same business service may be exposed through different interfaces.

A business interface may be part of a business role or actor through a composition relationship, and a business interface may serve a business role. A business interface may be assigned to one or more business services, which means that these services are exposed by the interface. The name of a business interface should preferably be a noun.

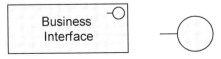

Figure 57: Business Interface Notation

8.2.5   Example

The "ArchiSurance Contact Center", modeled as a business actor, is composed of three employees, also modeled as business actors: "Greg", "Joan", and "Larry". The "ArchiSurance Contact Center" has three business interfaces to serve customers: "Phone", "E-mail", and "Web Chat". Greg fulfills the business role of "Travel Insurance Claim Analyst", Joan fulfills the business role of "Home Insurance Product Specialist", and Larry fulfills the business role of "Customer Service Representative". The former two business roles are specializations of a business role "Specialist". "High-Risk Claims Adjudication" is a business collaboration of two business roles: "Specialist" and "Customer Service Representative".

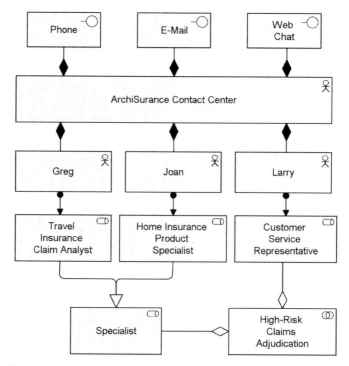

Example 23: Business Active Structure Elements

8.3   Behavior Elements

Based on service-orientation, a crucial design decision for the behavioral part of the ArchiMate metamodel is the distinction between "external" and "internal" behavior of an organization.

The externally visible behavior is modeled by the element *business service*. A business service represents a coherent piece of functionality that offers added value to the environment, independent of the way this functionality is realized internally. A distinction can be made between "external" business services, offered to external customers, and "internal" business services, offering supporting functionality to processes or functions within the organization.

Several types of internal behavior elements that can realize a service are distinguished. Although the distinction between the two is not always sharp, it is often useful to distinguish a *process view* and a *function view* on behavior; two elements associated with these views, *business process* and *business function*, are defined. Both elements can be used to group more detailed business processes/functions but based on different grouping criteria. A *business process* represents a workflow consisting of smaller processes/functions, with one or more clear starting points and leading to some result. It is sometimes described as "customer to customer", where this customer may also be an internal customer, in the case of sub-processes within an organization. The goal of such a business process is to "satisfy or delight the customer" [10]. A *business function* offers functionality that may be useful for one or more business processes. It groups behavior based on, required skills, resources, (application) support, etc. Typically, the business processes of an organization are defined based on the *products* and *services* that the organization offers, while the business functions are the basis for the assignment of resources to tasks and the application support.

A *business interaction* is a unit of behavior similar to a business process or function, but which is performed in a collaboration of two or more roles within the organization. Unlike the interaction concept in AMBER [9], which is an *atomic* unit of collaborative behavior, the ArchiMate business interaction can be decomposed into smaller interactions. Although interactions are external behavior from the perspective of the roles participating in the collaboration, the behavior is internal to the collaboration as a whole. Similar to processes or functions, the result of a business interaction can be made available to the environment through a business service.

A *business event* is something that happens and may influence business processes, functions, or interactions. The business event is similar to BPMN event, and to the initial state and final state elements in UML activity diagrams. However, the ArchiMate business event is more generally applicable in the sense that it can also be used to model other types of events, in addition to triggers.

In the Business Layer, three types of internal behavior element are defined: *business process*, *business function*, and *business interaction*.

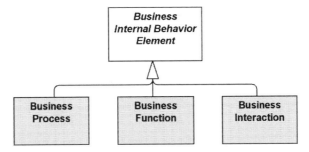

Figure 58: Business Internal Behavior Elements

Note: This figure does not show all permitted relationships; every element in the language can have composition, aggregation, and specialization relationships with elements of the same type. Furthermore, there are indirect relationships that can be derived, as explained in Section 5.7. The full specification of permitted relationships can be found in Appendix B.

8.3.1   Business Process

> A business process represents a sequence of business behaviors that achieves a specific result such as a defined set of products or business services.

A business process describes the internal behavior performed by a business role that is required to produce a set of products and services. For a consumer, the products and services are relevant, and the required behavior is merely a black box, hence the designation "internal".

A complex business process may be an aggregation of other, finer-grained processes. To each of these, finer-grained roles may be assigned.

There is a potential many-to-many relationship between business processes and business functions. Informally speaking, processes describe some kind of "flow" of activities, whereas functions group activities according to required skills, knowledge, resources, etc.

A business process may be triggered by, or trigger, any other business behavior element (e.g., business event, business process, business function, or business interaction). A business process may access business objects. A business process may realize one or more business services and may be served by business, application, or technology services. A business role may be assigned to a business process to perform this process manually. An automated business process can be realized by an application process. The name of a business process should clearly indicate a predefined sequence of actions using a verb or verb-noun combination and may include the word "process". Examples are "adjudicate claim", "employee on-boarding", "approval process", or "financial reporting".

In an ArchiMate model, the existence of business processes is depicted. High-level business, end-to-end processes, macro flows, and workflows can all be expressed with the same business process element in the ArchiMate language. It does not, however, list the flow of activities in detail. This is typically done during business process modeling, where a business process can be expanded using a business process design language; e.g., BPMN [12].

Figure 59: Business Process Notation

8.3.2 Business Function

A business function represents a collection of business behavior based on a chosen set of criteria such as required business resources and/or competencies, and is managed or performed as a whole.

Just like a business process, a business function also describes internal behavior performed by a business role. However, while a business process groups behavior based on a sequence or flow of activities that is needed to realize a product or service, a business function typically groups behavior based on required business resources, skills, competencies, knowledge, etc.

There is a potential many-to-many relation between business processes and business functions. Complex processes in general involve activities that offer various functions. In this sense, a business process forms a string of business functions. In general, a business function delivers added value from a business point of view. Organizational units or applications may coincide with business functions due to their specific grouping of business activities. Business functions are often closely aligned to an organization, but not necessarily explicitly governed by the organization.

Business functions can realize capabilities. Where business functions are often aligned with organization structure and describe the current, day-to-day activities of the enterprise, capabilities (see Section 7.3.1) represent its potential behavior and are independent from the implementation in the organization structure.

A business function may be triggered by, or trigger, any other business behavior element (business event, business process, business function, or business interaction). A business function may access business objects. A business function may realize one or more business services and may be served by business, application, or technology services. A business role may be assigned to a business function. The name of a business function should clearly indicate a well-defined behavior. Examples are customer management, claims administration, member services, recycling, or payment processing.

Figure 60: Business Function Notation

8.3.3 Business Interaction

A business interaction represents a unit of collective business behavior performed by (a collaboration of) two or more business actors, business roles, or business collaborations.

A business interaction is similar to a business process or function, but while a process or function may be performed by a single business active structure element, an interaction is performed by (a collaboration of) multiple active structure elements. These elements share the responsibility for performing the interaction.

A business interaction may be triggered by, or trigger, any other business behavior element (business event, business process, business function, or business interaction). A business interaction may access business objects. A business interaction may realize one or more business services and may use (internal) business services or application services. A business collaboration or two or more business actors or roles may be assigned to a business interaction. The name of a business interaction should preferably be a verb in the simple present tense.

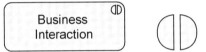

Figure 61: Business Interaction Notation

8.3.4 Business Event

A business event represents a business-related state change.

Business processes and other business behavior may be triggered or interrupted by a business event. Business processes may raise events that trigger other business processes, functions, or interactions. Unlike business processes, functions, and interactions, a business event is instantaneous: it does not have a duration. Events may originate from the environment of the organization (e.g., from a customer), as well as internal events generated by other processes within the organization.

A business event may have a time attribute that denotes the moment or moments at which the event happens. For example, this can be used to model time schedules; e.g., to model an event that triggers a recurring business process to execute every first Monday of the month.

A business event may trigger or be triggered (raised) by a business process, business function, or business interaction. A business event may access a business object and may be composed of other business events. The name of a business event should preferably be a verb in the perfect tense; e.g., "claim received".

Figure 62: Business Event Notation

8.3.5 Business Service

> A business service represents explicitly defined behavior that a business role, business actor, or business collaboration exposes to its environment.

A business service exposes the functionality of business roles or collaborations to their environment. This functionality is accessed through one or more business interfaces.

A business service should provide a unit of behavior that is meaningful from the point of view of the environment. It has a purpose which states this utility in terms of the value it delivers, and is modeled as a value element associated with the service. The environment includes the (behavior of) users from outside as well as inside the organization. Business services can be external, customer-facing services (e.g., a travel insurance service) or internal support services (e.g., a resource management service).

A business service may serve business, application, and technology behavior or active structure elements. A business process, business function, or business interaction may realize a business service. A business interface may be assigned to a business service. A business service may access business objects. The name of a business service should preferably be a verb ending with "-ing"; e.g., transaction processing. Also, a name explicitly containing the word "service" may be used.

Figure 63: Business Service Notation

8.3.6 Example

> "Claims Administration" is a business function that is composed of a number of business processes and a business interaction. This business function realizes a "Claims Processing" business service. A business event "Claim Filed" triggers the first business process "Accept Claim", which in turn triggers a business process "Assign Claim". Depending on the type of claim, either the business process "Adjudicate Standard Claim" or the business interaction "Adjudicate High-Risk Claim" is performed. Adjudication of high-risk claims is a business interaction because, according to the company policy, two people should always be involved in this activity to minimize the risk of fraud. After adjudication, the business processes "Notify Customer" and "Pay Claim" are performed in parallel, and when both have finished, business process "Close Claim" is triggered.

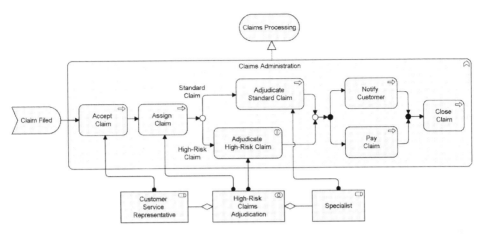

Example 24: Business Behavior Elements

8.4   Passive Structure Elements

The passive structure aspect of the Business Layer contains the passive structure elements (business objects) that are manipulated by behavior, such as business processes or functions. The passive entities represent the important concepts in which the business thinks about a domain.

In the Business Layer, there are two main types of passive structure elements: *business object* and *representation*. Furthermore, a contract, used in the context of a product, is a specialization of a business object.

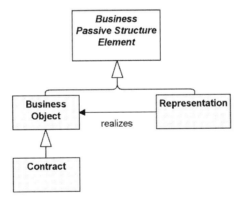

Figure 64: Business Passive Structure Elements

8.4.1   Business Object

> A business object represents a concept used within a particular business domain.

As explained in Section 3.6, the ArchiMate language in general focuses on the modeling of types, not instances, since this is the most relevant at the Enterprise Architecture level of description. Hence a business object typically models an object type (*cf.* a UML class) of which multiple instances may exist in operations. Only occasionally, business objects represent actual instances of information produced and consumed by behavior elements such as business processes. This is in particular the case for singleton types; i.e., types that have only one instance.

A wide variety of types of business objects can be defined. Business objects are passive in the sense that they do not trigger or perform processes. A business object could be used to represent information assets that are relevant from a business point of view and can be realized by data objects.

Business objects may be accessed (e.g., in the case of information objects, they may be created, read, or written) by a business process, function, business interaction, business event, or business service. A business object may have association, specialization, aggregation, or composition relationships with other business objects. A business object may be realized by a representation or by a data object (or both). The name of a business object should preferably be a noun.

Figure 65: Business Object Notation

8.4.2 Contract

> A contract represents a formal or informal specification of an agreement between a provider and a consumer that specifies the rights and obligations associated with a product and establishes functional and non-functional parameters for interaction.

The contract element may be used to model a contract in the legal sense, but also a more informal agreement associated with a product. It may also be or include an SLA describing an agreement about the functionality and quality of the services that are part of a product. A contract is a specialization of a business object.

The relationships that apply to a business object also apply to a contract. In addition, a contract may have an aggregation relationship with a product. The name of a contract is preferably a noun.

Figure 66: Contract Notation

8.4.3 Representation

> A representation represents a perceptible form of the information carried by a business object.

Representations (messages or documents) are the perceptible carriers of information that are related to business objects. If relevant, representations can be classified in various ways; for example, in terms of medium (electronic, paper, audio, etc.) or format (HTML, ASCII, PDF, RTF, etc.). A single business object can have a number of different representations as well as realize one or more specific business objects.

A meaning can be associated with a representation that carries this meaning. The name of a representation is preferably a noun.

Figure 67: Representation Notation

8.4.4   Example

The business object "Claim" may be realized by either of the following three physical representations (in different stages of the claims administration process): "Submission Form", "Claim File Summary", or "Claim Letter". All of these representations refer to a representation "Policy Summary", which realizes a contract "Insurance Policy".

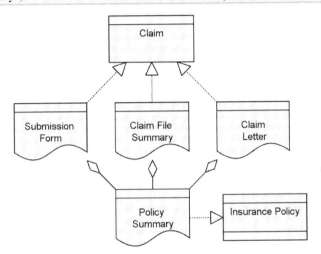

Example 25: Business Passive Structure Elements

8.5   Composite Elements

The Business Layer contains one composite element: *product*. This aggregates or composes services and passive structure elements across the layers of the ArchiMate core language.

Figure 68 shows the applicable part of the metamodel. This crosses layers, as also described in Chapter 11.

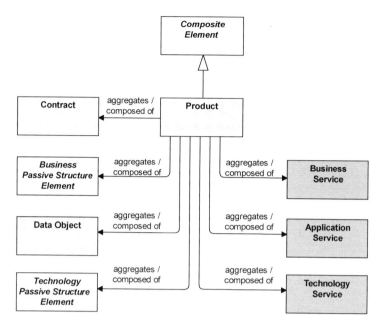

Figure 68: Product Metamodel

8.5.1   Product

A product represents a coherent collection of services and/or passive structure elements, accompanied by a contract, which is offered as a whole to (internal or external) customers.

This definition covers both intangible, services-based, or information products that are common in information-intensive organizations, as well as tangible, physical products. A financial or information product consists of a collection of services along with a contract that specifies the characteristics, rights, and requirements associated with the product. "Buying" a product gives the customer the right to use the associated services.

Generally, the product element is used to specify a product *type*. The number of product types in an organization is typically relatively stable compared to the processes that realize or support the products. "Buying" is usually one of the services associated with a product which results in a new instance of that product (belonging to a specific customer). Similarly, there may be services to modify or destroy a product.

A product may aggregate or compose business services, application services, technology services, business objects, data objects, and technology passive structure elements (artifacts and material), as well as a contract. Hence a product may aggregate or compose elements from other layers than the Business Layer.

A value may be associated with a product. The name of a product is usually the name used in the communication with customers, or possibly a more generic noun (e.g., "travel insurance").

Figure 69: Product Notation

8.5.2 Example

A product "Insurance" consists of a contract "Insurance Policy" and a business service "Customer Service", which aggregates four other business services: "Application", "Renewal", "Claims Processing", and "Appeal". An "Auto Insurance" product is a specialization of the generic "Insurance" product, with an additional business service "Drive Well and Save", and accompanying contract "Drive Well and Save Agreement".

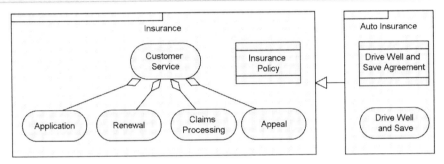

Example 26: Business Composite Element: Product

8.6 Summary of Business Layer Elements

Table 6 gives an overview of the Business Layer elements, with their definitions.

Table 6: Business Layer Elements

Element	Description	Notation	
Business Actor	Represents a business entity that is capable of performing behavior.	Business Actor	🧍
Business Role	Represents the responsibility for performing specific behavior, to which an actor can be assigned, or the part an actor plays in a particular action or event.	Business Role	
Business Collaboration	Represents an aggregate of two or more business internal active structure elements that work together to perform collective behavior.	Business Collaboration	

Element	Description	Notation
Business Interface	Represents a point of access where business services are made available to the environment.	Business Interface
Business Process	Represents a sequence of business behaviors that achieves a specific result such as a defined set of products or business services.	Business Process
Business Function	Represents a collection of business behavior based on a chosen set of criteria such as required business resources and/or competencies, and is managed or performed as a whole.	Business Function
Business Interaction	Represents a unit of collective business behavior performed by (a collaboration of) two or more business actors, business roles, or business collaborations.	Business Interaction
Business Event	Represents a business-related state change.	Business Event
Business Service	Represents explicitly defined behavior that a business role, business actor, or business collaboration exposes to its environment.	Business Service
Business Object	Represents a concept used within a particular business domain.	Business Object
Contract	Represents a formal or informal specification of an agreement between a provider and a consumer that specifies the rights and obligations associated with a product and establishes functional and non-functional parameters for interaction.	Contract
Representation	Represents a perceptible form of the information carried by a business object.	Representation
Product	Represents a coherent collection of services and/or passive structure elements, accompanied by a contract, which is offered as a whole to (internal or external) customers.	Product

9   Application Layer

The Application Layer elements are typically used to model the Application Architecture that describes the structure, behavior, and interaction of the applications of the enterprise.

9.1   Application Layer Metamodel

Figure 70 gives an overview of the Application Layer elements and their relationships. Whenever applicable, inspiration has been drawn from the analogy with the Business Layer.

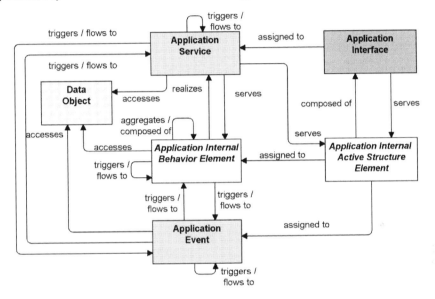

Figure 70: Application Layer Metamodel

Note: This figure does not show all permitted relationships; every element in the language can have composition, aggregation, and specialization relationships with elements of the same type. Furthermore, there are indirect relationships that can be derived, as explained in Section 5.7.

9.2   Active Structure Elements

The main active structure element for the Application Layer is the *application component*. This element is used to model any structural entity in the Application Layer: not just (re-usable) software components that can be part of one or more applications, but also complete software applications, sub-applications, or information systems. Although very similar to the UML component, the ArchiMate application component element strictly models the structural aspect of an application; its behavior is modeled by an explicit relationship to the behavior element.

The inter-relationships of components also form essential parts of the Application Architecture. Therefore, we also introduce the element of *application collaboration* here (see Figure 71).

defined as a collective of application components which perform application interactions. The element is very similar to the collaboration as defined in the UML standard [7], [8].

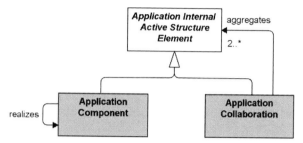

Figure 71: Application Internal Active Structure Elements

Note: This figure does not show all permitted relationships; every element in the language can have composition, aggregation, and specialization relationships with elements of the same type. Furthermore, there are indirect relationships that can be derived, as explained in Section 5.7.

In the purely structural sense, an *application interface* is the (logical) channel through which the services of a component can be accessed. In a broader sense (as used in, among others, the UML definition), an application interface defines some elementary behavioral characteristics: it defines the set of operations and events that are provided by the component. Thus, it is used to describe the functionality of a component. The application interface element can be used to model both *application-to-application* interfaces, which offer internal application services, and *application-to-business* interfaces (and/or *user interfaces*), which offer external application services.

9.2.1   Application Component

> An application component represents an encapsulation of application functionality aligned to implementation structure, which is modular and replaceable.

An application component is a self-contained unit. As such, it is independently deployable, re-usable, and replaceable. An application component performs one or more application functions. It encapsulates its behavior and data, exposes services, and makes them available through interfaces. Cooperating application components are connected via application collaborations.

An application component may be assigned to one or more application functions. An application component has one or more application interfaces, which expose its functionality. Application interfaces of other application components may serve an application component. The name of an application component should preferably be a noun.

The application component element is used to model entire applications (i.e., deployed and operational IT systems, as defined by the TOGAF framework [4]) and individual parts of such applications, at all relevant levels of detail. Application components can realize other application components. This is explained in Section 3.6.

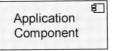

Figure 72: Application Component Notation

9.2.2   Application Collaboration

> An application collaboration represents an aggregate of two or more application internal active structure elements, that work together to perform collective application behavior.

An application collaboration specifies which application components or other application collaborations cooperate to perform a task. Collaborative behaviors similar to the communication pattern of these components are modeled by an application interaction. An application collaboration typically models a logical or temporary collaboration of application components and does not exist as a separate entity in the enterprise.

Application collaboration is a specialization of application internal active structure element, and aggregates two or more (cooperating) application components or other application collaborations. An application collaboration is an active structure element that may be assigned to one or more application interactions or other application internal behavior elements, which model the associated behavior. An application interface may serve an application collaboration which also may be composed of application interfaces. The name of an application collaboration should preferably be a noun.

Figure 73: Application Collaboration Notation

9.2.3   Application Interface

> An application interface represents a point of access where application services are made available to a user, another application component, or a node.

An application interface specifies how the functionality of a component can be accessed by other elements. An application interface exposes application services to the environment. The same application service may be exposed through different interfaces, and the same interface may expose multiple services.

In a sense, an application interface specifies a contract that a component making this interface available must fulfill. This may include parameters, protocols used, pre- and post-conditions, and data formats.

An application interface may be part of an application component through composition, which means that these interfaces are provided by that component and can serve other application components. An application interface can be assigned to application services, which means that the interface exposes these services to the environment. The name of an application interface should preferably be a noun.

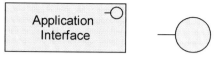

Figure 74: Application Interface Notation

9.2.4 Example

The "Online Travel Insurance Sales" application collaboration aggregates two application components: "Quotation" and "Purchase". The application collaboration provides an application interface "Web Services Interface" that serves another application component "Travel Website".

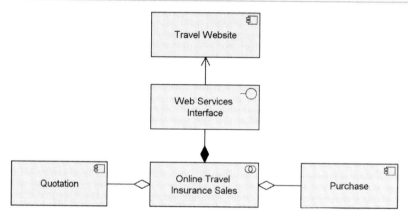

Example 27: Application Active Structure Elements

9.3 Behavior Elements

Behavior in the Application Layer is described in a way that is very similar to Business Layer behavior. As in the Business Layer, a distinction is made between the external behavior of application components in terms of *application services*, and the internal behavior of these components; e.g., *application functions* that realize these services.

An *application service* is an externally visible unit of behavior, provided by one or more components, exposed through well-defined interfaces, and meaningful to the environment. The service element provides a way to explicitly describe the functionality that components share with each other and the functionality that they make available to the environment. The concept fits well within service-oriented application architecture. The functionality that an interactive computer program provides through a user interface, is also modeled using an application service that is exposed by an application-to-business interface representing the user interface. Internal application services are exposed through an application-to-application interface.

An *application function* describes the internal behavior of a component needed to realize one or more application services. In analogy with the Business Layer, an *application process* models an ordering of application behavior, as a counterpart of a business process. Note that in most cases the internal behavior of a component is not modeled in too much detail in an architectural description. The description of such behavior may lead the architect to be confronted with detailed design issues.

An *application interaction* is the behavior of a collaboration of two or more application components. An application interaction is external behavior from the perspective of each of the participating components, but the behavior is internal to the collaboration as a whole.

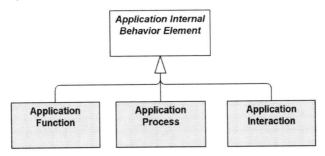

Figure 75: Application Internal Behavior Elements

Note: This figure does not show all permitted relationships; every element in the language can have composition, aggregation, and specialization relationships with elements of the same type. Furthermore, there are indirect relationships that can be derived, as explained in Section 5.7.

9.3.1 Application Function

An application function represents automated behavior that can be performed by an application component.

An application function describes the internal behavior of an application component. If this behavior is exposed externally, this is done through one or more services. An application function abstracts from the way it is implemented. Only the necessary behavior is specified.

An application function may realize one or more application services. Application services of other application functions and technology services may serve an application function. An application function may access data objects. An application component may be assigned to an application function (which means that the application component performs the application function). The name of an application function should preferably be a verb ending with "-ing"; e.g., "accounting".

Figure 76: Application Function Notation

9.3.2 Application Interaction

An application interaction represents a unit of collective application behavior performed by (a collaboration of) two or more application components.

An application interaction describes the collective behavior that is performed by the components that participate in an application collaboration. This may, for example, include the communication pattern between these components. An application interaction can also specify the joint behavior needed to realize an application service. The details of the interaction between the application components involved in an application interaction can be expressed during the detailed application design using, for example, a UML interaction diagram.

An application collaboration of two or more individual application components may be assigned to an application interaction. An application interaction may realize application services. Business services, application services, and technology services may serve an application interaction. An application interaction may access data objects. The name of an application interaction should clearly identify a series of application behaviors; e.g., "client profile creation" or "update customer records".

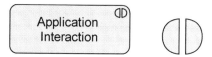

Figure 77: Application Interaction Notation

9.3.3 Application Process

> An application process represents a sequence of application behaviors that achieves a specific result.

An application process describes the internal behavior performed by an application component that is required to realize a set of services. For a (human or automated) consumer the services are relevant, and the required behavior is merely a black box, hence the designation "internal".

An application process may realize application services. Other application services may serve (be used by) an application process. An application process may access data objects. An application component may be assigned to an application process (which means that this component performs the process). The name of an application process should clearly identify a series of application behaviors using a verb or verb-noun combination; e.g., "claims adjudication process", or "general ledger update job".

Figure 78: Application Process Notation

9.3.4 Application Event

> An application event represents an application state change.

Application functions and other application behavior may be triggered or interrupted by an application event. Also, application behavior may raise events that trigger other application behavior. Unlike processes, functions, and interactions, an event is instantaneous; it does not have duration. Events may originate from the environment of the organization (e.g., from an external application), but also internal events may occur generated by, for example, other applications within the organization.

An application event may have a time attribute that denotes the moment or moments at which the event happens. For example, this can be used to model time schedules; e.g., an event that triggers a daily batch process.

An application event may trigger or be triggered (raised) by an application function, process, or interaction. An application event may access a data object and may be composed of other application events. The name of an application event should preferably be a verb in the perfect tense; e.g., "claim received".

Figure 79: Application Event Notation

9.3.5 Application Service

An application service represents an explicitly defined exposed application behavior.

An application service exposes the functionality of components to their environment. This functionality is accessed through one or more application interfaces and is realized by one or more application functions that are performed by the component. It may require, use, and produce data objects.

An application service should be meaningful from the point of view of the environment; it should provide a unit of behavior that is, in itself, useful to its users. It has a purpose that states this utility to the environment in terms of the value it delivers, modeled as a value element associated with the service. This means that if this environment includes business processes, application services should have business relevance.

An application service may serve business, application, and technology behavior or active structure elements. An application function or process may realize an application service. An application interface may be assigned to an application service. An application service may access data objects. The name of an application service should preferably be a verb ending with "-ing"; e.g., "transaction processing". Also, a name explicitly containing the word "service" may be used.

Figure 80: Application Service Notation

9.3.6 Example

The "Purchase Travel Insurance" application function is composed of two other application functions: "Transfer Quotation", realizing an application service "Get Quotation", and "Finalize Purchase", realizing an application service "Purchase Quoted Insurance". These application functions model the behavior of the "Quotation" and "Purchase" application components of Example 27. An application event "Request for a Quotation" triggers an application process "Obtain Travel Insurance", which is served by the two aforementioned application services.

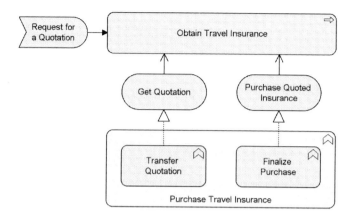

Example 28: Application Behavior Elements

9.4 Passive Structure Elements

The passive counterpart of the application component in the Application Layer is called a *data object*. This element is used in the same way as data objects (or object types) in well-known data modeling approaches, most notably the "class" concept in UML class diagrams. A data object can be seen as a representation of a business object, as a counterpart of the representation element in the Business Layer. The ArchiMate language does not define a specific layer for information; however, elements such as business objects and data objects are used to represent the information entities and also the logical data components that realize the business objects.

9.4.1 Data Object

A data object represents data structured for automated processing.

A data object should be a self-contained piece of information with a clear meaning to the business, not just to the application level. Typical examples of data objects are a customer record, a client data set, or an insurance claim.

As explained in Section 3.6, the ArchiMate language in general focuses on the modeling of types, not instances, since this is the most relevant at the Enterprise Architecture level of description. Hence a data object typically models a logical object type of which one or many instances may exist in operational applications.

An application function or process can operate on data objects. A data object may be communicated via interactions and used or produced by application services. A data object can be accessed by an application function, application interaction, or application service. A data object may realize a business object and may be realized by an artifact. A data object may have association, specialization, aggregation, or composition relationships with other data objects. The name of a data object should preferably be a noun.

Figure 81: Data Object Notation

Example

An "Online Insurance Quotation" data object is composed of three other data objects: "Quoted Price", "Terms and Conditions", and "Certificate of Authenticity". "Auto Insurance Quotation" and "Travel Insurance Quotation" are two specializations of the "Online Insurance Quotation" data object. "Travel Insurance Quotation" contains an additional data object "Purchased Itinerary".

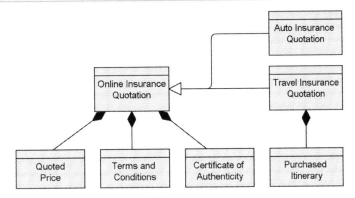

Example 29: Application Passive Structure Elements

9.5　Summary of Application Layer Elements

Table 7 gives an overview of the Application Layer elements, with their definitions.

Table 7: Application Layer Elements

Element	Definition	Notation
Application Component	Represents an encapsulation of application functionality aligned to implementation structure, which is modular and replaceable.	
Application Collaboration	Represents an aggregate of two or more application internal active structure elements that work together to perform collective application behavior.	
Application Interface	Represents a point of access where application services are made available to a user, another application component, or a node.	

Element	Definition	Notation
Application Function	Represents automated behavior that can be performed by an application component.	Application Function
Application Interaction	Represents a unit of collective application behavior performed by (a collaboration of) two or more application components.	Application Interaction
Application Process	Represents a sequence of application behaviors that achieves a specific result.	Application Process
Application Event	Represents an application state change.	Application Event
Application Service	Represents an explicitly defined exposed application behavior.	Application Service
Data Object	Represents data structured for automated processing.	Data Object

10 Technology Layer

The Technology Layer elements are typically used to model the Technology Architecture of the enterprise, describing the structure and behavior of the technology infrastructure of the enterprise.

The physical elements are an extension to the Technology Layer for modeling the physical world. They only include active and passive structure elements; no specific physical behavior elements are defined. Physical technology elements can be combined with other technology elements (such as device) and be part of the same node, to model an integrated piece of operational and information technology.

10.1 Technology Layer Metamodel

Figure 82 gives an overview of the Technology Layer elements and their relationships. Whenever applicable, inspiration is drawn from the analogy with the Business and Application Layers. In the following sections, several more elements will be introduced.

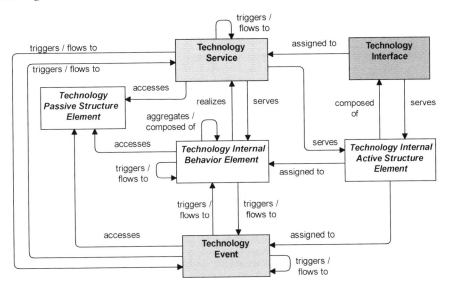

Figure 82: Technology Layer Metamodel

Note: This figure does not show all permitted relationships; every element in the language can have composition, aggregation, and specialization relationships with elements of the same type. Furthermore, there are indirect relationships that can be derived, as explained in Section 5.7.

10.2 Active Structure Elements

The main active structure element for the Technology Layer is the *node*. This element is used to model structural entities in this layer. It strictly models the structural aspect of a system: its behavior is modeled by an explicit relationship to a behavior element.

A *technology interface* is the (logical) place where the technology services offered by a node can be accessed by other nodes or by application components from the Application Layer.

Nodes can consist of information and technology elements modeled as *devices* and *system software*, and also of physical technology elements modeled as facilities and equipment (see Section 10.6). A *device* models a physical computational resource, upon which artifacts may be deployed for execution. *System software* is an infrastructural software component running on a device. Typically, a node consists of a number of sub-nodes; for example, a device such as a server and system software to model the operating system.

The inter-relationships of components in the Technology Layer are mainly formed by the communication infrastructure. The *path* models the relation between two or more technology internal active structure elements, through which these can exchange information. The physical realization of a path is modeled with a *communication network*; i.e., a physical communication medium between two or more devices (or other networks).

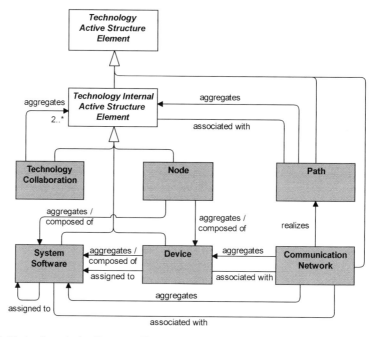

Figure 83: Technology Active Structure Elements

Note: This figure does not show all permitted relationships; every element in the language can have composition, aggregation, and specialization relationships with elements of the same type. Furthermore, there are indirect relationships that can be derived, as explained in Section 5.7.

10.2.1   Node

A node represents a computational or physical resource that hosts, manipulates, or interacts with other computational or physical resources.

The Open Group Standard (2022)

Nodes are active structure elements that perform technology behavior and execute, store, and process artifacts or materials. For instance, nodes are used to model application platforms, defined by the TOGAF framework [4] as: *"a collection of technology components of hardware and software that provide the services used to support applications"*.

Nodes can be interconnected by paths and may be assigned to an artifact to model that the artifact is deployed on the node.

The name of a node should preferably be a noun. A node may consist of sub-nodes.

Artifacts deployed on a node may either be drawn inside the node or connected to it with an assignment relationship.

Figure 84: Node Notation

10.2.2   Device

A device represents a physical IT resource upon which system software and artifacts may be stored or deployed for execution.

A device represents a physical IT resource with processing capability. It is typically used to model hardware systems such as mainframes, PCs, smartphones, or routers. It can also be used to model virtualized hardware, e.g., in an IaaS environment. Usually, devices are part of a node together with system software. Devices may be composite; i.e., consist of sub-devices.

Devices can be interconnected by communication networks as well as being assigned to artifacts and to system software, to model deployment on that device. A node can contain one or more devices.

The name of a device should preferably be a noun phrase referring to the type of hardware; e.g., "IBM System z mainframe".

Figure 85: Device Notation

10.2.3   System Software

System software represents software that provides or contributes to an environment for storing, executing, and using software or data deployed within it.

System software is used to model the software environment in which artifacts run. This can be, an operating system, a JEE application server, a database system, or a workflow engine. System software can also be used to represent communication middleware. Usually, system software is combined with a device representing the hardware environment to form a general node.

A device or system software can be assigned to other system software; e.g., to model different layers of software running on top of each other. System software can be assigned to artifacts to model that these artifacts are deployed on that software and can realize other system software. A node can be composed of or aggregate system software.

The name of system software should preferably be a noun referring to the type of execution environment; e.g., "JEE server". System software may be composed of other system software; e.g., an operating system containing a database.

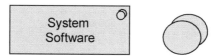

Figure 86: System Software Notation

10.2.4   Technology Collaboration

A technology collaboration represents an aggregate of two or more technology internal active structure elements that work together to perform collective technology behavior.

A technology collaboration specifies which technology internal active structure elements and/or other technology collaborations cooperate to perform some task. The collaborative behavior, including the communication pattern of these elements, is modeled by a technology interaction. A technology collaboration typically models a logical or temporary collaboration of technology internal active structure elements and does not exist as a separate entity in the enterprise.

Technology collaboration is a specialization of technology internal active structure element, and aggregates two or more (cooperating) technology internal active structure elements. A technology collaboration is an internal active structure element that may be assigned to one or more technology interactions, or to other technology internal behavior elements that model the associated behavior. A technology interface may serve a technology collaboration, and a technology collaboration may be composed of technology interfaces. The name of a technology collaboration should preferably be a noun.

Figure 87: Technology Collaboration Notation

10.2.5   Technology Interface

A technology interface represents a point of access where technology services offered by a technology internal active structure element can be accessed.

A technology interface specifies how the technology services of a technology internal active structure element can be accessed by other elements. A technology interface exposes a technology service to the environment. The same service may be exposed through different interfaces.

In a sense, a technology interface specifies a kind of contract that a node realizing this interface must fulfill. This may include, parameters, protocols used, pre- and post-conditions, and data formats.

A technology interface may be part of a technology internal active structure through composition, which means that these interfaces are provided by that element and can serve other elements. A technology interface can be assigned to a technology service, to expose that service to the environment.

The name of a technology interface should preferably be a noun.

Figure 88: Technology Interface Notation

Note: In previous versions of this standard, this element was called "infrastructure interface". This usage is still permitted but deprecated and will be removed from a future version of the standard.

10.2.6   Path

A path represents a link between two or more technology internal active structure elements, through which these elements can exchange data, energy, or material.

A path is used to model the logical communication (or distribution) relations between technology internal active structure elements. It is realized by one or more communication networks (or distribution networks when modeling physical elements; see Section 10.6.3), which represent the physical communication (or distribution) links. The properties (e.g., bandwidth, latency) of a path are usually aggregated from these underlying networks.

A path connects two or more technology internal active structure elements. A path is realized by one or more networks. A path can aggregate nodes.

Figure 89: Path Notation

10.2.7   Communication Network

A communication network represents a set of structures that connects devices or system software for transmission, routing, and reception of data.

A communication network represents the physical communication infrastructure. It *"provides the basic services to interconnect systems and provide the basic mechanisms for opaque transfer of data. It contains the hardware and software elements which make up the networking and physical communications links used by a system, and of course all the other systems connected to the network"*, as described by the TOGAF Series Guide: The TOGAF Technical Reference Model (TRM) [19].

A communication network connects two or more devices or system software. The most basic communication network is a single link between two devices, but it may comprise multiple links and associated network equipment or software. A network has properties such as bandwidth and latency. A communication network realizes one or more paths. It embodies the physical realization of the logical path between nodes.

A communication network can consist of sub-networks. It can aggregate devices and system software to model the routers, switches, and firewalls that are part of the network infrastructure.

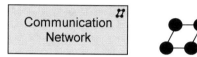

Figure 90: Communication Network Notation

Note: Formerly, this element was called "network". This usage is still permitted but deprecated and will be removed from a future version of the standard.

10.2.8   Example

Two "Blade System" devices are connected to a communication network "Data Center Network". This in turn is connected to another communication network "Wide Area Network" through a node "Data Center Switch". The two communication networks together realize a path "Data Replication Path". Both "Blade System" devices and the "Data Center Switch" node have a technology interface "Management Interface". Device "Blade System 1" deploys "Hypervisor" system software for hardware virtualization. Two system software components are deployed on the "Hypervisor": an "Open Source Operating System" and a "Proprietary Operating System", creating two virtual hosts, modeled as nodes "Quotation Virtual Host" and "Purchase Virtual Host".

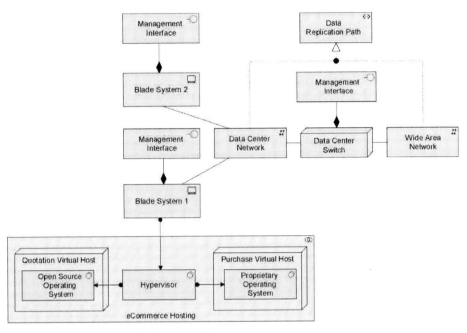

Example 30: Technology Active Structure Elements

10.3 Behavior Elements

Behavior elements in the Technology Layer are similar to the behavior elements in the other layers. As in the Business and Application Layers, a distinction is made between the external behavior of technology internal active structure elements in terms of *technology services*, and the internal behavior of these elements; i.e., *technology functions*, *technology processes*, and *technology interactions* that realize these services.

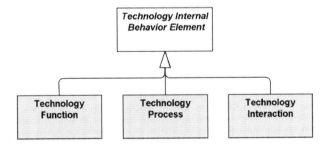

Figure 91: Technology Internal Behavior Elements

10.3.1 Technology Function

A technology function represents a collection of technology behavior that can be performed by a technology internal active structure element.

A technology function describes the internal behavior of a technology internal active structure element; for the user of an element that performs a technology function, this function is invisible. If its behavior is exposed externally, this is done through one or more technology services. A technology function abstracts from the way it is implemented. Only the necessary behavior is specified.

A technology function may realize technology services. A technology function may access technology passive structure elements. An internal active structure element may be assigned to a technology function (which means that the node performs the technology function). The name of a technology function should preferably be a verb ending with "-ing".

Figure 92: Technology Function Notation

Note: In previous versions of this standard, this element was called "infrastructure function". This usage is still permitted but deprecated and will be removed from a future version of the standard.

10.3.2   Technology Process

> A technology process represents a sequence of technology behaviors that achieves a specific result.

A technology process describes internal behavior of a technology internal active structure element; for the user of that element, this process is invisible. If its behavior is exposed externally, this is done through one or more technology services. A technology process abstracts from the way it is implemented. Only the necessary behavior is specified. It can access technology passive structure elements as input and use or transform these to produce other technology passive structure elements as output.

A technology process may realize technology services and other technology services may serve (be used by) a technology process. A technology internal active structure element may be assigned to a technology process, which means that this element performs the process. The name of a technology process should clearly identify a series of technology behaviors using a verb or verb-noun combination; e.g., "Boot up system" or "Replicate database".

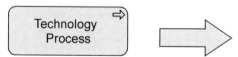

Figure 93: Technology Process Notation

10.3.3   Technology Interaction

> A technology interaction represents a unit of collective technology behavior performed by (a collaboration of) two or more technology internal active structure elements.

A technology interaction describes the collective behavior that is performed by two or more technology internal active structure elements, possibly via their participation in a technology collaboration. This may include the communication pattern between these elements. A technology interaction can also specify the joint behavior needed to realize a technology service. The details of the interaction between the technology internal active structure elements involved in a technology interaction, can be expressed during the detailed design using a UML interaction diagram.

A technology collaboration, or two or more nodes, may be assigned to a technology interaction. A technology interaction may realize technology services and technology services may serve a technology interaction. A technology interaction may access artifacts. The name of a technology interaction should clearly identify a collective technology behavior; e.g., "client profile creation" or "update customer records".

Figure 94: Technology Interaction Notation

10.3.4 Technology Event

A technology event represents a technology state change.

Technology functions and other technology behavior may be triggered or interrupted by a technology event. Technology functions may raise events that trigger other technology behavior. Unlike processes, functions, and interactions, an event is instantaneous: it does not have a duration. Events may originate from the environment of the organization, but also internal events may occur generated by other devices within the organization.

A technology event may have a time attribute that denotes the moment or moments at which the event happens. For example, this can be used to model time schedules; e.g., to model an event that triggers a recurring infrastructure function such as making a daily backup.

A technology event may trigger or be triggered (raised) by a technology function, process, or interaction. A technology event may access an artifact or material and may be composed of other technology events. The name of a technology event should preferably be a verb in the perfect tense; e.g., "message received".

Figure 95: Technology Event Notation

10.3.5 Technology Service

A technology service represents an explicitly defined exposed technology behavior.

A technology service exposes the functionality of a technology internal active structure element to its environment. This functionality is accessed through one or more technology interface and may require, use, and produce artifacts.

A technology service should be meaningful from the point of view of the environment; it should provide a unit of behavior that is, in itself, useful to its users, such as application components and nodes. This added value can be modeled as a value element associated with the service.

Typical technology services may include messaging, storage, naming, and directory services. It may access artifacts; e.g., a file containing a message.

A technology service may serve business, application components, and technology behavior or active structure elements . A technology service is realized by a technology function, process, or interaction. A technology service is exposed by a technology internal active structure element by assigning technology interfaces to it. A technology service may access artifacts. A technology service may consist of sub-services.

The name of a technology service should preferably be a verb ending with "-ing"; e.g., "messaging". Also, a name explicitly containing the word "service" may be used.

Figure 96: Technology Service Notation

Note: In previous versions of this standard, this element was called "infrastructure service". This usage is still permitted but deprecated and will be removed from a future version of the standard.

10.3.6   Example

A technology event "Database Update" triggers a technology process "Replicate Remote Data", which is served by a technology service "Database Update Replication". This technology service is realized by a technology function "Database Replication", which is composed of four other technology functions: "Administrate Replication", "Handle Local Updates", "Handle Remote Updates", and "Monitor Replication Status". There are information flows from the "Administrate Replication" technology function to the other three technology functions.

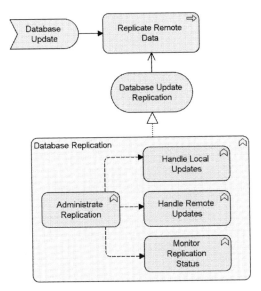

Example 31: Technology Behavior Elements

10.4 Passive Structure Elements

Technology passive structure elements model the passive structure elements that are used and processed by the infrastructure. Technology passive structure elements represent the informational and physical objects manipulated by the infrastructure of an enterprise. They are abstract elements; i.e., they are not instantiated in models but serve as the generic type of the things manipulated by the Technology Layer. This may include both artifacts (e.g., files) and physical material.

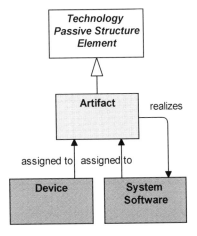

Figure 97: Technology Passive Structure Elements

Technology passive structure elements may be accessed by technology behavior (functions, processes, interactions, events, and services). A technology passive structure elements may have association, specialization, aggregation, or composition relationships with other technology passive structure elements. It may be an artifact (see Section 10.4.1) or material (see Section 10.7.1). Specific technology internal active structure elements may be assigned to technology passive structure elements. For example, a device may be assigned to an artifact, modeling the deployment of the artifact on that device.

10.4.1 Artifact

An artifact represents a piece of data that is used or produced in a software development process, or by deployment and operation of an IT system.

An artifact represents a "physical" element in the IT world. Artifact is a specialization of technology passive structure elements. It is typically used to model (software) products such as source files, executables, scripts, database tables, messages, documents, specifications, and model files. It can be accessed (created, deleted, read, written) by technology behavior elements. An instance (copy) of an artifact can be deployed on a device or system software; this is modeled with an assignment relationship. An artifact could be used to represent a physical data component that realizes a data object.

An application component or system software may be realized by one or more artifacts. A data object may be realized by one or more artifacts. A device or system software element may be assigned to an artifact to model that the artifact is deployed on this element. Thus, the two typical ways to use the artifact element are as an *execution component* or as a *data file*. In fact, these could be defined as specializations of the artifact element.

The name of an artifact should preferably be the name of the file it represents; e.g., "order.jar". An artifact may consist of sub-artifacts.

Figure 98: Artifact Notation

10.4.2 Example

A "Web Archive" artifact (which may realize an application component) is composed of two other artifacts: "Database Access Java Archive" and "Business Logic Java Archive". Two specializations of the "Web Archive" artifact are a "Purchase Application Web Archive" and a "Quotation Application Web Archive". A "Travel Insurance Database" artifact (which may realize a data object) is associated with the "Web Archive" artifact.

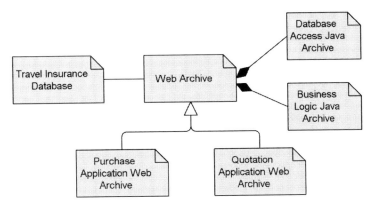

Example 32: Technology Passive Structure Element: Artifact

10.5 Physical Elements Metamodel

Figure 99 gives an overview of the physical elements and their relationships.

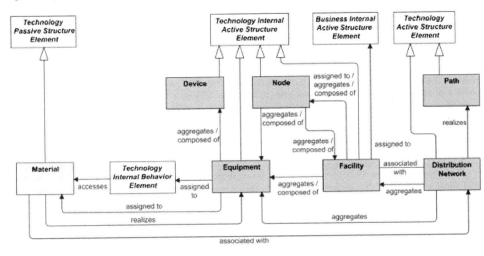

Figure 99: Physical Elements Metamodel

Note: This figure does not show all permitted relationships; every element in the language can have composition, aggregation, and specialization relationships with elements of the same type. Furthermore, there are indirect relationships that can be derived, as explained in Section 5.7.

10.6 Physical Active Structure Elements

The *equipment* element is the main active structure element within the physical elements. This element is used to model structural entities in this layer. It is used to model any physical machinery, tools, instruments, or implements. It strictly models the structural aspect of a system;

its behavior is modeled by an explicit relationship to the behavior elements. The *facility* active structure element is used to model the environment in which this equipment is used; for example, office buildings, factories, laboratories, or data centers.

The inter-relationships of physical elements are mainly formed by the logistics infrastructure. The path element from the Technology Layer models the relation between two or more nodes, through which these nodes can exchange information or material. The physical realization of a path is modeled with a *distribution network*; i.e., a physical connection between two or more pieces of equipment (or other physical networks). This can be used to model, for example, rail or road networks, the water supply, power grid, or gas network.

10.6.1   Equipment

> Equipment represents one or more physical machines, tools, or instruments that can create, use, store, move, or transform materials.

Equipment comprises all active processing elements that carry out physical processes in which materials are used or transformed. It is possible to model nodes that are formed by a combination of IT infrastructure (devices, system software) and physical infrastructure (equipment); e.g., an MRI scanner at a hospital, a production plant with its control systems, etc.

Material can be accessed (e.g., created, used, moved, transformed, or otherwise manipulated) by equipment. Equipment may be assigned to material in order to model where the material is stored. Material may realize equipment. Equipment can serve other equipment as well as other active structure elements such as business roles and actors, and facilities can be assigned to equipment. A piece of equipment can be composed of other pieces of equipment or devices. Facilities can be assigned to equipment (i.e., equipment is installed and used in or on a facility). Equipment can be aggregated in a location.

The name of a piece of equipment should preferably be a noun.

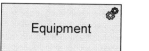

Figure 100: Equipment Notation

10.6.2   Facility

> A facility represents a physical structure or environment.

A facility represents a physical resource that has the capability of facilitating (e.g., housing or locating) the use of equipment. It is typically used to model factories, buildings, or outdoor constructions that have an important role in production or distribution processes. Examples of facilities include a factory, laboratory, warehouse, shopping mall, cave, or spaceship. Facilities may be composite; i.e., consist of sub-facilities.

Facilities can be interconnected by distribution networks. A facility can serve other facilities and other active structure elements such as business roles and actors. A facility can be composed of other facilities or nodes and can be aggregated in a location.

The name of a facility should preferably be a noun referring to the type of facility; e.g., "Rotterdam oil refinery".

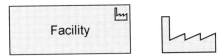

Figure 101: Facility Notation

10.6.3 Distribution Network

A distribution network represents a physical network used to transport materials or energy.

A distribution network represents the physical distribution or transportation infrastructure. It embodies the physical realization of the logical paths between facilities.

A distribution network connects two or more facilities and may realize one or more paths. A distribution network can consist of sub-networks and can aggregate facilities and equipment to model railway stations and trains that are part of a rail network.

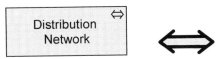

Figure 102: Distribution Network Notation

10.7 Passive Structure Elements

10.7.1 Material

Material represents tangible physical matter or energy.

Material is typically used to model raw materials and physical products, and also energy sources such as fuel and electricity. Material can be accessed by technology behavior elements to model how it is created, used, moved, transformed, or otherwise manipulated. Equipment may be assigned to material, to model where the material is stored. This allows you to model the distinction between, for instance, "the sand is in the dump truck" and "the sand is poured into the concrete mixer". Material may realize equipment.

The name of material should be a noun. Pieces of material may be composed of other pieces of material.

Figure 103: Material Notation

10.8   Example

An "Assembly Line", modeled as equipment and installed at a facility "Manufacturing Plant", makes use of materials "Pre-Assembled Circuit Board", "Internal Antenna", and "Plastic Case" to produce material "Vehicle Telematics Appliance". The appliance is subsequently transported from the "Manufacturing Plant" to the facilities "National Distribution Center", and from there to the "Local Distribution Center". These are connected via the distribution networks "Overseas Shipping" and "Local Trucking". These distribution networks together realize the path "Intermodal Freight".

Note that in a life-size architecture model, you may want to split this up into multiple views; for example, one that shows the production of the "Vehicle Telematics Appliance" from the input materials, a second that shows the material flows between the plant and the distribution centers, and a third that focuses in on the transportation modalities between these facilities.

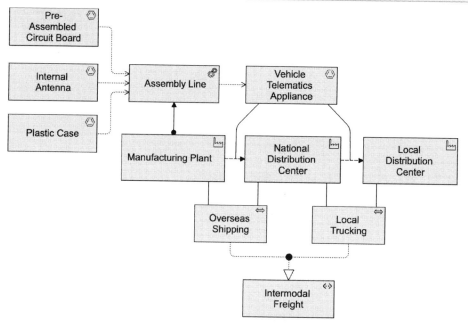

Example 33: Physical Elements

10.9   Summary of Technology Layer Elements

Table 8 gives an overview of the Technology Layer elements, with their definitions.

Table 8: Technology Layer Elements

Element	Definition	Notation
Node	Represents a computational or physical resource that hosts, manipulates, or interacts with other computational or physical resources.	
Device	Represents a physical IT resource upon which system software and artifacts may be stored or deployed for execution.	
System Software	Represents software that provides or contributes to an environment for storing, executing, and using software or data deployed within it.	
Technology Collaboration	Represents an aggregate of two or more technology internal active structure elements that work together to perform collective technology behavior.	
Technology Interface	Represents a point of access where technology services offered by a technology internal active structure can be accessed.	
Path	Represents a link between two or more technology internal active structure elements, through which these elements can exchange data, energy, or material.	
Communication Network	Represents a set of structures that connects devices or system software for transmission, routing, and reception of data.	
Technology Function	Represents a collection of technology behavior that can be performed by a technology internal active structure element.	
Technology Process	Represents a sequence of technology behaviors that achieves a specific result.	

Element	Definition	Notation
Technology Interaction	Represents a unit of collective technology behavior performed by (a collaboration of) two or more technology internal active structure elements.	Technology Interaction
Technology Event	Represents a technology state change.	Technology Event
Technology Service	Represents an explicitly defined exposed technology behavior.	Technology Service
Artifact	Represents a piece of data that is used or produced in a software development process, or by deployment and operation of an IT system.	Artifact
Equipment	Represents one or more physical machines, tools, or instruments that can create, use, store, move, or transform materials.	Equipment
Facility	Represents a physical structure or environment.	Facility
Distribution Network	Represents a physical network used to transport materials or energy.	Distribution Network
Material	Represents tangible physical matter or energy.	Material

11 Relationships Between Core Layers

The previous chapters have presented the concepts to model the Business, Application, and Technology Layers of an enterprise. However, a central issue in Enterprise Architecture is business-IT alignment: how can these layers be matched? This chapter describes the relationships that the ArchiMate language offers to model the link between business, applications, and technology.

11.1 Alignment of the Business Layer and Lower Layers

Figure 104 shows the relationships between the Business Layer, the Application Layer, and the Technology Layer elements. There are two main types of relationships between these layers:

1. *Serving* relationships; for example, between application service and the different types of business behavior elements, and between application interface and business role; *vice versa*, serving relationships between business service and application behavior elements, and between business interface and application component. These relationships represent the behavioral and structural aspects of the support of the business by applications.

2. *Realization* relationships; for example, from an application process or function to a business process or function, or from a data object or a technology passive structure element to a business object, to indicate that the data object is a digital representation of the corresponding business object, or the technology element is a physical representation of the business object. Note that there is no realization of business internal active structure elements by application or technology elements because people cannot be realized by applications or technology. Instead, the business behavior of those active structure elements can be realized by application or technology behavior elements, to which in turn application or technology active structure elements can be assigned.

In addition, there may be an aggregation relationship between a product and an application or technology service, and a data or technology passive structure element, to indicate that these services or objects can be offered directly to a customer as part of the product.

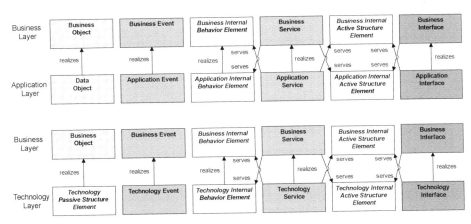

Figure 104: Relationships Between Business Layer and Application and Technology Layer Elements

Note: This figure does not show all permitted relationships; there are indirect relationships that can be derived, as explained in Section 5.7.

11.2   Alignment of the Application and Technology Layers

Figure 105 shows the relationships between Application Layer and Technology Layer elements. There are two types of relationships between these layers:

1.   *Serving* relationships, between technology service and the different types of application behavior elements, and between technology interface and application component; *vice versa*, serving relationships between application service and technology behavior, and application interface and technology internal active structure element. These relationships represent the behavioral and structural aspects of the use of technology infrastructure by applications and *vice versa*.

2.   *Realization* relationships from technology process or function to application process or function, from artifact to data object, to indicate that the data object is realized by, for example, a physical data file, from artifact to application component, to indicate that a physical data file is an executable that realizes an application or part of an application. (Note: In this case, an artifact represents a "physical" component that is deployed on a device or system software element; this is modeled with an assignment relationship. A (logical) application component is realized by an artifact and, indirectly, by the element on which the artifact is deployed.)

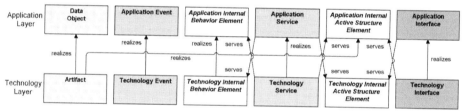

Figure 105: Relationships Between Application Layer and Technology Layer Elements

Note: This figure does not show all permitted relationships; there are indirect relationships that can be derived, as explained in Section 5.7.

Due to the derived relationships that are explained in Section 5.7, it is also possible to draw relationships directly between the Business and Technology Layers. For example, if a business object is realized by a data object, which in turn is realized by an artifact, this artifact indirectly realizes the business object.

11.3   Example

Example 34 shows how the cross-layer relationships integrate the different layers, and how this can be depicted in one view. It also shows how the optional notation with letters in the upper-left corner is used to distinguish between layers.

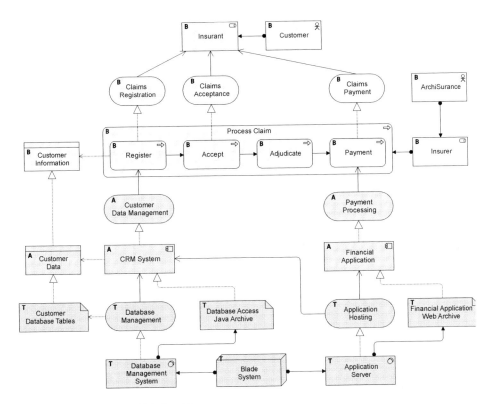

Example 34: Cross-Layer Relationships

12 Implementation and Migration Layer

The implementation and migration elements support the implementation and migration of architectures. This includes modeling implementation programs and projects to support program, portfolio, and project management. It also includes support for migration planning.

12.1 Implementation and Migration Elements Metamodel

Figure 106 gives an overview of the implementation and migration elements and their relationships.

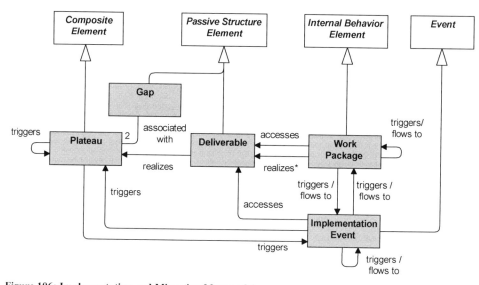

Figure 106: Implementation and Migration Metamodel

Note: This figure does not show all permitted relationships; every element in the language can have composition, aggregation, and specialization relationships with elements of the same type. Furthermore, there are indirect relationships that can be derived, as explained in Section 5.7.

The realization relationship from Work Package to Deliverable (marked with an asterisk in the figure) is deprecated and may be removed in a future version of the standard. It is recommended to use an access relationship instead.

12.2 Implementation and Migration Elements

12.2.1 Work Package

> A work package represents a series of actions identified and designed to achieve specific results within specified time and resource constraints.

The central behavioral element is a *work package*. A work package is typically not a continuously ongoing activity, but has a start and an end. These may be modeled as attributes. It produces a well-defined set of results, typically modeled as goals, outcomes, or deliverables. The work package element can be used to model sub-projects or tasks within a project, complete projects, programs, or project portfolios. In an Agile context, a work package can be used to model the work performed in an Agile iteration (e.g., sprint) or higher level increment.

Figure 107: Work Package Notation

Conceptually, a work package is similar to a business process, in that it consists of a set of causally-related tasks, aimed at producing a well-defined result. However, a work package is a unique "one-off" process. Still, a work package can be described in a way very similar to the description of a process.

12.2.2 Deliverable

A deliverable represents a precisely defined result of a work package.

Work packages produce *deliverables*. These may be results of any kind; e.g., reports, papers, services, software, physical products, etc., or intangible results such as organizational change. A deliverable may also be the implementation of (a part of) an architecture.

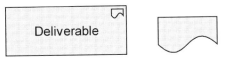

Figure 108: Deliverable Notation

Often, deliverables are contractually specified and in turn formally reviewed, agreed, and signed off by the stakeholders as is, for example, prescribed by the TOGAF framework [4].

12.2.3 Implementation Event

An implementation event represents a state change related to implementation or migration.

Work packages may be triggered or interrupted by an implementation event. Also, work packages may raise events that trigger other behavior. Unlike a work package, an event is instantaneous: it does not have a duration.

An implementation event may have a time attribute that denotes the moment or moments at which the event happens. For example, this can be used to model project schedules and milestones; e.g., an event that triggers a work package, an event that denotes its completion (with a triggering relationship from the work package to the event), or an event that denotes a lifecycle change of a deliverable (via an access relationship to that deliverable).

Implementation events access deliverables to fulfill project objectives. For example, in a project to deliver a completely new application along with the technology needed to host it, an implementation event "release to production" could access the deliverables "final build", "staging environment", and "production environment".

An implementation event may trigger or be triggered (raised) by a work package or a plateau. An implementation event may access a deliverable and may be composed of other implementation events.

An implementation event may be associated with any core element; e.g., to indicate a lifecycle state change. The name of an implementation event should preferably be a verb in the perfect tense; e.g., "project initiation phase completed".

Figure 109: Implementation Event Notation

12.2.4   Plateau

A plateau represents a relatively stable state of the architecture that exists during a limited period of time.

An important premise in the TOGAF framework is that the various architectures are described for different stages in time. In each of the Phases B, C, and D of the ADM, Baseline and Target Architecture descriptions are created, describing the current situation and the desired future situation. In Phase E (Opportunities and Solutions), so-called Transition Architectures are defined, showing the enterprise at incremental states reflecting periods of transition between the Baseline and Target Architectures. Transition Architectures are used to allow for individual work packages and projects to be grouped into managed portfolios and programs, illustrating the business value at each stage and expressing the step-by-step approach to migration.

In order to support this, the *plateau* element is defined.

Figure 110: Plateau Notation

12.2.5   Gap

A gap represents a statement of difference between two plateaus.

The *gap* element is associated with two plateaus (e.g., Baseline and Target Architectures, or two consecutive Transition Architectures) and represents the differences between these plateaus.

In the TOGAF framework [4], a gap is an important outcome of a gap analysis in Phases B, C, and D of the ADM process, and forms an important input for the subsequent implementation and migration planning.

Figure 111: Gap Notation

12.2.6   Example

The "Next Generation Services Program" work package is composed of three other work packages. An implementation event "Program Approved" triggers the first work package, "Architecture and Planning", which triggers the work package "Application Services Layer Development", which triggers the work package "Business Services Development", which triggers the implementation event "Program Completed". The "Program Approved" implementation event also provides a deliverable "Program Brief", as input for the first work package. Work package "Architecture and Planning" realizes three deliverables: "Business Plan", "Architecture", and "Roadmap" (which is accessed by the "Application Services Layer Development" work package), which collectively realize the plateau "Strategic Plan Complete". This plateau follows the initial plateau "Baseline", filling the gap "Knowledge of How to Address Customer Needs". Similarly, the other work packages realize other deliverables that realize the subsequent plateaus.

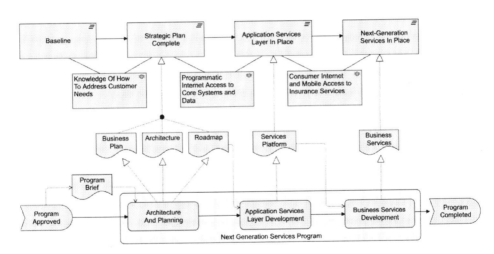

Example 35: Implementation and Migration Elements

12.3   Summary of Implementation and Migration Elements

Table 9 gives an overview of the implementation and migration elements, with their definitions.

Table 9: Implementation and Migration Elements

Element	Definition	Notation
Work Package	Represents a series of actions identified and designed to achieve specific results within specified time and resource constraints.	Work Package
Deliverable	Represents a precisely defined result of a work package.	Deliverable
Implementation Event	Represents a state change related to implementation or migration.	Implementation Event
Plateau	Represents a relatively stable state of the architecture that exists during a limited period of time.	Plateau
Gap	Represents a statement of difference between two plateaus.	Gap

12.4   Relationships

The implementation and migration elements use the standard ArchiMate relationships.

12.5   Relationships with Other Aspects and Layers

Figure 112 shows how the implementation and migration elements can be related to the ArchiMate core elements.

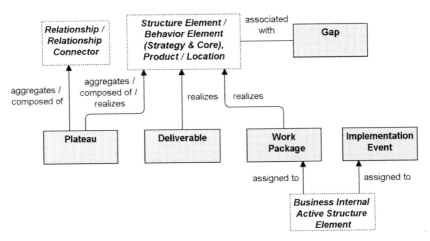

Figure 112: Relationships of Implementation and Migration Elements with Core Elements

A business internal active structure element may be assigned to a work package. This is used to model, for instance, a Project Manager business role that is responsible for the work package.

A plateau is linked to an architecture that is valid for a certain time span. To indicate which parts of the architecture belong to a certain plateau, a plateau may aggregate or compose any of the concepts of the ArchiMate core language. Realization from a plateau to part of the architecture is also permitted. For example, a capability may be realized by a plateau, signifying that a certain capability increment is valid only during the time span of that plateau.

A gap is associated with the core concepts that are unique to one of the plateaus linked by the gap; i.e., the core concepts that make up the difference between these plateaus.

A deliverable may realize, among others, the implementation of an architecture or a part of an architecture. Therefore, any of the concepts of the ArchiMate core language may be linked to a deliverable by means of a realization relationship.

Like most of the core language concepts, a composite element may aggregate a work package or deliverable.

Weaker relationships may also be defined. For example, the association relationship may be used to show that parts of the architecture are affected in some way by certain work packages.

Strictly speaking, the relationships between the implementation and migration elements and the motivation elements are indirect relationships; e.g., a deliverable realizes a requirement or goal through the realization of an ArchiMate core element (e.g., an application component, business process, or service). However, it is still useful to make these relationships explicit to show that a deliverable is needed to realize certain requirements and goals.

Also, motivation elements can be related to a certain plateau; e.g., certain requirements may only be applicable to the Target Architecture, while others may apply to a certain Transition Architecture. Similarly, plateaus can be used for capability-based planning. This can be modeled by means of the aggregation or composition relationships.

Figure 113 summarizes the relationships between implementation and migration elements and motivation elements. Goals, outcomes, and requirements can be aggregated or composed in plateaus. Requirements can be realized by deliverables. Since outcomes and goals can be realized by requirements, they can of course be realized indirectly by deliverables as well.

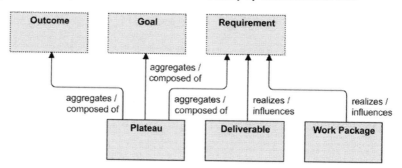

Figure 113: Relationships of Implementation and Migration Elements with Motivation Elements

13 Stakeholders, Architecture Views, and Viewpoints

13.1 Introduction

Establishing and maintaining a coherent Enterprise Architecture is clearly a complex task, because it involves many different people with differing backgrounds using various notations. In order to get a handle on this complexity, researchers have initially focused on the definition of architectural frameworks for classifying and positioning the various architectural descriptions with respect to each other (e.g., the Zachman framework [5], [8]).

Architecture frameworks provide general guidance to deliver Architecture Descriptions along with a process. The ArchiMate language, as a modeling notation, provides a detailed insight into the structure and coherence of different architectures, so its use complements and supports architecture frameworks.

The ArchiMate language provides a flexible approach in which architects and other stakeholders can use their own views on the Enterprise Architecture. In this approach, architecture views are specified by architecture viewpoints. Architecture viewpoints define abstractions on the set of models representing the Enterprise Architecture, each aimed at a particular type of stakeholder and addressing a particular set of concerns. Viewpoints can be used to view certain aspects in isolation, and to relate two or more aspects.

In the domain of Enterprise Architecture, the TOGAF framework describes a taxonomy of architecture views for different categories of stakeholders. In addition to this description of views, the TOGAF framework also provides guidelines for the development and use of architecture viewpoints and views in Enterprise Architecture models.

The architecture viewpoints and views proposed by any of the above-mentioned frameworks should not be considered in isolation: views are inter-related and, often, it is exactly a combination of views together with their underlying inter-dependency relationships that is the best way to describe and communicate a piece of architecture. It should, however, be noted that viewpoints and views have a limiting character. They are eventually a restriction of the whole system (and architecture) to a partial number of aspects – a view is just a partial incomplete depiction of the system.

13.2 Stakeholders and Concerns

This chapter introduces a method for using the ArchiMate language to systematically address stakeholder concerns, the *viewpoint mechanism*. This viewpoint mechanism conforms to the ISO/IEC 42010 standard [14], which provides a model for Architecture Description. Stakeholders, concerns, viewpoints, and views are important elements in this model, as depicted in Figure 114.

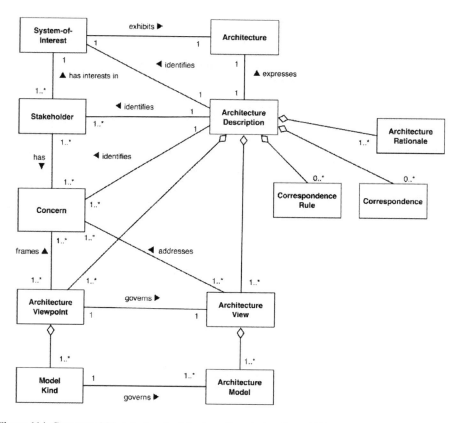

Figure 114: Conceptual Model of an Architecture Description (from [14])

The ArchiMate language with the viewpoint mechanism described in Section 13.4 assists and guides the architect in definition and classification of governing viewpoints. The architect will use this mechanism in his work to construct and design views for stakeholder communication.

13.3   Architecture Views and Viewpoints

Architecture views are an ideal mechanism to purposefully convey information about architecture areas. In general, a view is defined as a part of an Architecture Description that addresses a set of related concerns and is tailored for specific stakeholders. A view is specified by means of an architecture viewpoint, which prescribes the concepts, models, analysis techniques, and visualizations that are provided by the view. Simply put, a view is what you see, and a viewpoint is where you are looking from.

An Architecture Description includes one or more architecture views. An architecture view (or simply "view") addresses one or more of the concerns held by a stakeholder of the system.

An architecture view expresses the architecture of the system of interest in accordance with an architecture viewpoint (or simply "viewpoint"). There are two aspects to a viewpoint: the concerns it frames for the stakeholders and the conventions it establishes on views.

An architecture viewpoint frames one or more concerns. A concern can be framed by more than one viewpoint.

A view is governed by its viewpoint: the viewpoint establishes the conventions for constructing, interpreting, and analyzing the view to address concerns framed by that viewpoint. Viewpoint conventions can include languages, notations, model kinds, design rules and/or modeling methods, analysis techniques, and other operations on views.

Architecture viewpoints are a means to focus on particular aspects and layers of the architecture. These aspects and layers are determined by the concerns of a stakeholder with whom communication takes place. What should and should not be visible from a specific viewpoint is therefore entirely dependent on the argumentation with respect to a stakeholder's concerns.

Viewpoints are designed for the purpose of communicating certain aspects and layers of an architecture. The communication enabled by a viewpoint can be strictly informative, but in general is bi-directional. The architect informs stakeholders, and stakeholders give their feedback (critique or consent) on the presented aspects and layers. What is and what is not shown in an architecture view depends on the scope of the viewpoint and on what is relevant to the concerns of the stakeholder. Ideally, these are the same; i.e., the viewpoint is designed with specific concerns of a stakeholder in mind. Relevance to a stakeholder's concern, therefore, is the selection criterion that is used to determine which elements and relationships are to appear in a view.

13.4   Viewpoint Mechanism

An architect is confronted with many different types of stakeholders and concerns. To help in selecting the right viewpoints for the task at hand, we introduce a framework for the definition and classification of viewpoints: the *viewpoint mechanism*. The framework is based on two dimensions: purpose and content. Figure 115 shows how the viewpoint mechanism is used to create views addressing stakeholder concerns.

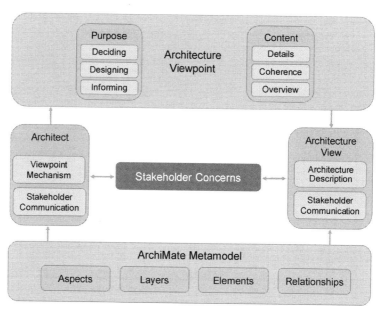

Figure 115: Framing Stakeholder Concerns using the Viewpoint Mechanism

The architect communicates with the stakeholder to understand and document their concerns. The viewpoint mechanism is used to identify purpose and content and to help define and classify the viewpoint. The viewpoint governs the construction and design of the view. The view is a description of the architecture addressing stakeholder concerns and is governed by the viewpoint.

Creating an ArchiMate viewpoint consists of two steps:

1. Selecting a subset of relevant concepts (elements and relationships) from the ArchiMate metamodel, based on the information that is needed to address the stakeholder's concerns.

2. Defining a representation to depict these concepts in a way that is understood by the stakeholders. This can be a diagram that uses standard or customized ArchiMate notation, a catalog of elements, a matrix showing the relationships between two groups of elements, or an entirely different visualization.

Applying this viewpoint to an architecture model means that those parts of the architecture are selected that match the chosen set of concepts (Step 1) and are depicted in the manner prescribed by Step 2.

13.4.1 Defining and Classifying Viewpoints

To help define and classify viewpoints based on a repeatable structure, the ArchiMate language assists the architect in selecting purpose and content relevant for the stakeholder's concerns.

The purpose dimension is supported by the following three categories:

*   *Designing*: design viewpoints support architects and designers in the design process from initial sketch to detailed design

    Typically, design viewpoints consist of diagrams.

- *Deciding*: decision support viewpoints assist managers in the process of decision-making by offering insight into cross-domain architecture relationships, typically through projections and intersections of underlying models, but also by means of analytical techniques

  Typical examples are cross-reference tables, landscape maps, lists, and reports.

- *Informing*: informing viewpoints help to inform any stakeholder about the Enterprise Architecture, in order to achieve understanding, obtain commitment, and convince adversaries

  Typical examples are illustrations, animations, cartoons, flyers, etc.

The content dimension uses the ArchiMate Core Framework to select relevant aspects and layers. This is supported by the following three categories:

- *Details*: views on the detailed level typically consider one layer and one aspect from the ArchiMate Core Framework

  Typical stakeholders are a software engineer responsible for design and implementation of a software component or a process owner responsible for effective and efficient process execution.

- *Coherence*: at the coherence abstraction level, multiple layers or multiple aspects are spanned

  Extending the view to more than one layer or aspect enables the stakeholder to focus on architecture relationships like process-uses-system (multiple layer) or application-uses-object (multiple aspect). Typical stakeholders are operational managers responsible for a collection of IT services or business processes.

- *Overview*: the overview abstraction level addresses both multiple layers and multiple aspects

  Typically, such overviews are addressed to Enterprise Architects and decision-makers, such as CEOs and CIOs.

13.4.2 Creating the View

With a governing viewpoint, the architect can create and design a view. The view contains elements and relationships (concepts) from the ArchiMate metamodel. The architect can design and create an appropriate representation for these elements and relationships, suitable for the stakeholder(s) and concern(s) being framed. The architect may use the profile mechanism described in Section 14.1 to create representations based on attributes of elements and relationships; for example, to create color-coded heat maps. The view does not have to be visual or graphical in nature.

13.5 Example Viewpoints

See Appendix C for a set of example viewpoints.

14   Language Customization Mechanisms

Every specific purpose and usage of an architecture modeling language brings about its own specific demands on the language. Yet, it should be possible to use a language for only a limited, though non-specific, modeling purpose. Therefore, the ArchiMate language, specified in the ArchiMate metamodel and described in Chapter 4 to Chapter 12, contains only the basic elements and relationships that serve general Enterprise Architecture modeling purposes. However, the language should also be able to facilitate, through customization[2] mechanisms, specialized, or domain-specific purposes, such as:

- Support for specific types of model analysis

- Support for the communication of architectures

- Capture the specifics of a certain application domain (e.g., the financial sector)

The argument behind this statement is to provide a means to allow customization of the language that is tailored towards such specific domains or applications, without burdening the language with a lot of additional concepts and notations which most people would barely use. The remainder of this chapter is devoted to the customization mechanisms that are part of the ArchiMate language, and to a series of illustrative examples of such customizations.

14.1   Adding Attributes to ArchiMate Concepts

As stated earlier in this standard, the ArchiMate language contains only the elements and relationships that are necessary for general architecture modeling. However, users might want to perform model-based performance or cost calculations to attach supplementary information (textual, numerical, etc.) to the model concepts. Every concept in an ArchiMate model can have attributes attached to it. ArchiMate concepts can be enriched in a generic way with supplementary information by means of a "profiling" specialization mechanism (see also [9]).

A *profile* is a data structure which can be defined separately from the ArchiMate language but can be dynamically coupled with concepts; i.e., the user of the language is free to decide whether and when the assignment of a profile to a model concept is necessary. Profiles are specified as sets of typed attributes. Each of these attributes may have a default value that can be changed by the user.

Two types of profiles can be distinguished:

- *Pre-defined profiles*: these are profiles that have a predefined attribute structure and can be implemented beforehand in any tool supporting the ArchiMate language

  Examples of such profiles are sets of attributes for ArchiMate concepts that have to be specified in order to execute common types of analysis.

- *User-defined profiles:* through a profile definition language, the user is able to define new profiles, thus extending the definition of ArchiMate elements or relationships with supplementary attribute sets.

---

[a] Note that this chapter was called Language Extension Mechanisms in previous versions of this standard. Since these customization mechanisms do not actually *extend* the language, it was decided to rename this chapter and these mechanisms.

At least the following basic data types are allowed for these attributes:

- String
- Integer
- Real
- Boolean
- Currency
- Date
- URL

In addition, the following complex types are supported:

- Structure, consisting of one or more fields of a basic type
- List, consisting of elements of one of the other types

The ArchiMate Model Exchange File Format [20] defines how these types are encoded and exchanged.

Examples

Table 10 shows possible profiles with input attributes needed for certain types of cost and performance analysis of architecture models [13]. Each "serving" relationship may have a weight (indicating the average number of uses); each (business, application, or technology) "service" may have fixed and variable costs and an (average) service time; and each structure element (e.g., business role, business actor, application component, device) may have fixed and variable costs and a capacity.

Table 10: Profile Examples

"Serving" Profile		"Service" Profile		"Structure Element" Profile	
Attribute	Type	Attribute	Type	Attribute	Type
Weight	Real	Fixed cost	Currency	Fixed cost	Currency
		Variable cost	Currency	Variable cost	Currency
		Service time	Time	Capacity	Integer

Table 11 shows a generic profile that can be used to model cardinalities and role labels of relationships.

Table 11: Relationship Profile Example

Cardinality and Relation Roles Profile	
Attribute	**Type**
'From' cardinality	Structure (lower bound, upper bound), e.g. 0..0, 0..1, 0..*, 1..*
'To' cardinality	Structure (lower bound, upper bound)
'From' relation role	String
'To' relation role	String

14.2 Specialization of Concepts

Specialization is a simple and powerful way to define new elements or relationships based on the existing ones. Specialized elements inherit the properties of their generalized elements (including the relationships that are allowed for the element), but some of the relationships that apply to the specialized element need not be allowed for the generalized element. Also, new graphical notation could be introduced for a specialized concept, but preferably with a resemblance to the notation of the generalized concept; e.g., by adding an icon or other graphical marker, or changing the existing icon. A specialized element or relationship strongly resembles a stereotype as it is used in UML. The stereotype notation with angled brackets may also be used to denote a specialized concept. Finally, for a specialized concept, certain attributes may be predefined, as described in the previous section.

Specialization of relationships is also allowed. Similar to specialization of elements, a specialized relationship inherits all properties of its "parent" relationship, with possible additional restrictions. For example, two specializations of the assignment relationship may be used to model responsibility *versus* accountability. Another example is a specialization of the flow relationship to model material flow in a supply chain.

Specialization of concepts provides extra flexibility as it allows organizations or individual users to customize the language-to their own preferences and needs, while the underlying precise definition of the concepts is preserved. This also implies that analysis and visualization techniques developed for the ArchiMate language still apply when the specialized concepts are used.

Specialization of concepts is done by using the profile mechanism described in Section 14.1. The name of the profile is the name of the specialization, and it may have other attributes if relevant to the specialization. The specialized concept is modeled by assigning such a profile to the general concept.

The profile may also define a specific notation to denote the specialization. The default is the guillemet notation of UML for stereotypes ("«specialization name»"). Other options include specific icons, colors, fonts, or symbols. Note that multiple specialization profiles may be assigned to the same generalized concept; in the default notation, these are shown as a comma-separated list ("«specialization 1, specialization 2»").

14.2.1 Examples of Specializations of Business Layer Elements (Informative)

Table 12 shows examples of specializations of Business Layer concepts.

Table 12: Example Specializations of Business Layer Elements

Parent Concept	Specialized Concept	Description
Business Actor	Individual	A natural person capable of performing behavior in the context of an enterprise.
	Organizational Unit	Any named subdivision of an organization (e.g., a department).
	Organization	An entity such as an institution, corporation, or association that has a collective goal and is linked to an external environment.
	Threat Agent	Anything (e.g., an object, substance, individual, or group) that is capable of acting against an asset in a manner that can result in harm. This can be intentional; i.e., an attacker, but also unintentional; e.g., a well-intentioned, but inept, computer operator who trashes a daily batch job by typing the wrong command.
Business Service	Business Decision	A conclusion that a business arrives at through business logic and which the business is interested in managing.
Business Collaboration	Social Network	A social structure made up of social actors (individuals or organizations) and the connections between these actors.
Business Process	Business Activity	Atomic internal behavior element (at the considered abstraction level) that will not be decomposed any further.
Business Event	Threat Event (Risk & Security Overlay)	Event with the potential to adversely impact an asset. An *attack* is a specific type of threat event that is the result of an intentional malicious activity of an attacker, which is a specific type of threat agent.
	Loss Event (Risk & Security Overlay)	Any circumstance that causes a loss or damage to an asset.

14.2.2 Examples of Specializations of Application Layer Elements (Informative)

Table 13 shows examples of specializations of Application Layer elements.

Table 13: Example Specializations of Application Layer Elements

Parent Concept	Specialized Concept	Description
Application Component	Logical Application Component	An encapsulation of application functionality that is independent of a particular implementation.
	Physical Application Component	An application, application module, application service, or other deployable component of functionality.
Application Interface	Application-to-Application Interface	Interface that is used to communicate between application components.

Parent Concept	Specialized Concept	Description
	Graphical User Interface	On-screen interface (GUI) with which a human user can interact with an application component.

14.2.3 Examples of Specializations of Technology Layer Elements (Informative)

Table 14 shows examples of specializations of Technology Layer elements.

Table 14: Example Specializations of Technology Layer Elements

Parent Concept	Specialized Concept	Description
Node	Logical Technology Component	An encapsulation of technology infrastructure that is independent of a particular product. A class of technology product.
	Physical Technology Component	A specific technology infrastructure product or technology infrastructure product instance.
Device	Mobile Device	A portable device such as a smartphone or tablet.
	Embedded Device	A computing device that is part of a piece of equipment.
Network	Wi-Fi Network	Wireless Local Area Network (WLAN).
	Wide Area Network	Long-range data communication network.
Technology Service	Processing Service	Service used for processing data by a node.
	Storage Service	Service used for storing data on a node, typically offered by a database or file system.
	Communication Service	Service used for transporting information (e.g., voice, data) between nodes.

14.2.4 Examples of Specializations of Physical Elements (Informative)

Table 15 shows examples of specializations of physical elements.

Table 15: Example Specializations of Physical Elements

Parent Concept	Specialized Concept	Description
Equipment	Vehicle	A movable piece of equipment used for transportation purposes.
	Train	A vehicle intended for use on a rail network.
Facility	Factory	A large-scale physical resource used for receipt, temporary storage, and redistribution of goods.
Material	Ore	Rock containing minerals, raw material in mining, and related industries.

Parent Concept	Specialized Concept	Description
	Building Material	Material used in building and construction such as concrete, bricks and mortar, beams, and girders, etc.
	Fuel	Material used as an energy source in, for example, production or transportation.
Distribution Network	Rail Network	Network for rail transport, on which trains are used.
	Energy Grid	Network for distribution of energy, such as an electrical power grid or a gas distribution network.

14.2.5 Examples of Specializations of Motivation Elements (Informative)

Table 16 shows examples of specializations of motivation elements.

Table 16: Example Specializations of Motivation Elements

Parent Concept	Specialized Concept	Description
Driver	Metric	The extent, quantity, amount, or degree of something, as determined by measurement or calculation.
Assessment	Vulnerability (Risk & Security Overlay)	The probability that an asset will be unable to resist the actions of a threat agent.
	Risk (Risk & Security Overlay)	The probable frequency and probable magnitude of future loss.
Goal	Business Objective	A time-bound milestone for an organization used to demonstrate progress towards a goal.
	Control Objective (Risk & Security Overlay)	Aim or purpose of specified control measures which address the risks that these control measures are intended to mitigate.
Principle	Business Policy	A directive that is not directly enforceable, whose purpose is to govern or guide the enterprise.
Requirement	Control Measure (Risk & Security Overlay)	An action, device, procedure, or technique that reduces a threat, a vulnerability, or an attack by eliminating or preventing it, by minimizing the harm it can cause, or by discovering and reporting it so that corrective action can be taken.
	Business Rule	An enforceable directive intended to govern, guide, or influence business behavior.

Example 36 illustrates the use of specializations of Business Layer and motivation elements to model the results of a risk analysis, and the control objectives and required control measures to mitigate the identified risks. This example uses the UML stereotype notation with angled brackets to denote specialized elements.

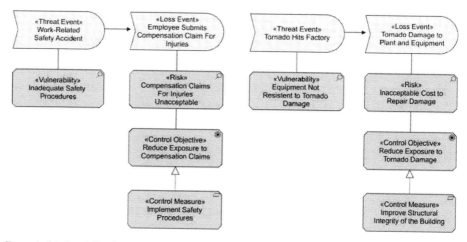

Example 36: Specializations of Business Layer and Motivation Elements

14.2.6 Examples of Specializations of Strategy Elements (Informative)

Table 17 shows examples of specializations of strategy elements.

Table 17: Example Specializations of Strategy Elements

Parent Concept	Specialized Concept	Description
Capability	Capability Increment	A specialization of a capability realized by a specific plateau or a state in the architecture that represents a stage in the evolution of that capability.
Course of Action	Strategy	A high-level, broad-scope approach to achieve a long-term goal.
	Tactic	A narrow-scope approach to achieve a short-term goal, used to detail a strategy.

14.2.7 Examples of Specializations of Implementation and Migration Elements (Informative)

Table 18 shows examples of specializations of implementation and migration elements.

Table 18: Example Specializations of Implementation and Migration Elements

Parent Concept	Specialized Concept	Description
Work Package	Program	A coordinated set of projects that deliver business benefits to the organization.
	Project	A time- and resource-bound activity that delivers specific business benefits to an organization.

14.2.8 Examples of Specializations of Composite Elements (Informative)

Table 19 shows examples of specializations of compound elements. In addition to the specialization of single model elements, grouping can also be used to define specific *compound* elements.

Table 19: Example Specializations of Composite Elements

Parent Concept	Specialized Concept	Description
Grouping	Risk Domain (Risk & Security Overlay)	A domain consisting of entities that share one or more characteristics relevant to risk management or security. A risk domain is also a context or set of conditions that affects a risk exposure level.
Grouping of Application Component, Application Function, and Data Object	Data Store	A repository for persistently storing and managing collections of data.

14.2.9 Examples of Specializations of Relationships and Relationship Connectors (Informative)

Table 20 shows examples of specializations of relationships and relationship connectors.

Table 20: Example Specializations of Relationships and Relationship Connectors

Parent Concept	Specialized Concept	Description
Flow	Money Flow	A flow of money between behavior elements.
Assignment	Responsibilities Assignment	Assignment from a business actor to a business role.
	Behavior Assignment	Assignment from an active structure to a behavior element.
Or-junction	Or-join	A junction with two or more incoming triggering and one outgoing triggering relationship, representing that at least one of the incoming relationships must be triggered to trigger the outgoing one.

A   Summary of Language Notation

This appendix describes the default iconography of the ArchiMate language. Modelers can choose to use a different iconography on any diagram if it helps to communicate better with stakeholders. However, it is recommended to use the default iconography so that teams using the ArchiMate language have a collective understanding of the view being developed. Conforming tools shall at least support these notations.

A.1   Core Elements

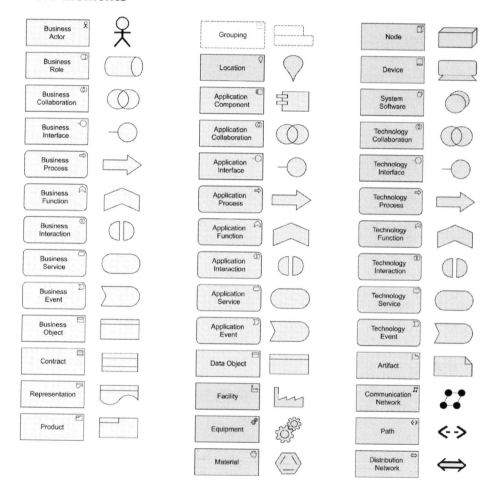

A.2   Motivation, Strategy, Implementation and Migration Elements

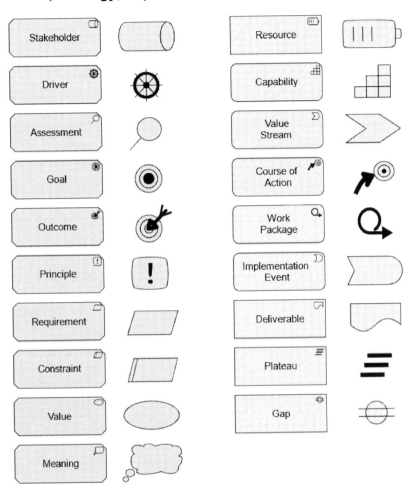

A.3 Relationships and Relationship Connectors

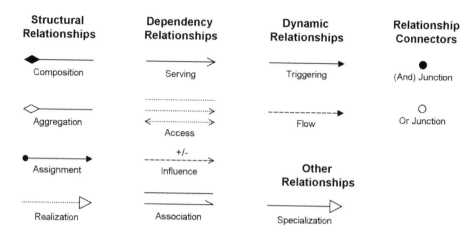

Structural Relationships	Dependency Relationships	Dynamic Relationships	Relationship Connectors
Composition	Serving	Triggering	(And) Junction
Aggregation	Access	Flow	Or Junction
Assignment	Influence	**Other Relationships**	
Realization	Association	Specialization	

B   Relationships (Normative)

This appendix details the normative requirements for relationships between elements of the ArchiMate modeling language. This is mainly intended for tool implementation purposes.

B.1   Specification of Derivation Rules

The following sections specify the formal rules for deriving relationships. The input relationships used for derivation must be allowed by the tables in this appendix. The resulting relationship will then always be allowed by definition and is listed in these tables as well. Note that these derivation rules do not work on relationships between core elements and other elements such as motivation, strategy, or implementation and migration elements, with the exception of the realization and influence relationships. This appendix states in more detail the restrictions that were applied to the use of the derivation rules to arrive at the relationship tables. Applying these rules and restrictions together results in the tables in this appendix, which contain all allowed relationships in the language.

We distinguish between two types of derivations: those that are certainly true in any model where these rules apply, and those that are potentially true but uncertain, depending on the specifics of the model concerned.

> **Notation of Derivation Rules**
>
> In the description of the derivation rules, a shorthand is used to describe relations: $p(a,b){:}R$ is used to describe the relationship with name p that has concept a as source, concept b as target, and R as its relationship type.
>
> The source and target concepts may be of any type. The relationship type can be restricted by the definition.
>
> By convention, concepts are named a, b, and c in order of appearance, relationships are named p, q, and r in order of appearance, and relationship types are named S, T, and U in order of appearance.

B.2   Derivation Rules for Valid Relationships

This section states the derivation rules for derivations that are valid in any model where these rules apply.

B.2.1   Valid Derivations for Specialization Relationships

DR 1: Transitivity of Specialization

> If two relationships $p(a,b){:}S$ and $q(b,c){:}S$ exist, with S being *Specialization*, then a relationship $r(a,c){:}S$ can be derived.

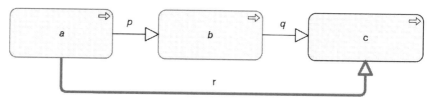

Example 37: Transitivity of Specialization

B.2.2 Valid Derivations for Structural Relationships

The structural relationships can be ordered by "strength":

- Realization (weakest)
- Assignment
- Aggregation
- Composition (strongest)

Part of the language definition is an abstraction rule that states that, two structural relationships that join at an intermediate element under specific conditions, can be combined and replaced by the weaker of the two.

DR 2: Derivation Between Structural Relationships

> If two relationships $p(a,b){:}S$ and $q(b,c){:}T$ exist, with S and T being structural relationships, then a relationship $r(a,c){:}U$ can be derived, with U being the weakest of S and T.

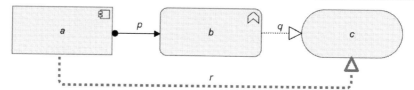

Example 38: Derivation of Structural Relationships

Informally, this means that if two structural relationships are "in line" (the target of one relation joins at the source of the other relation) they can be replaced by the weakest of the two. Transitively applying this property allows us to replace a "chain" of structural relationships that are in line (with intermediate model elements) by the weakest structural relationship in the chain.

An example is shown in Example 39: assume that the goal is to omit the functions, sub-functions, and services from the model. In this case, an indirect realization relationship (the relationship labeled "Derived Relationship" (thick arrow on the right) can be derived from "Financial Application" to the "Payment Service" (from the chain assignment – composition – realization).

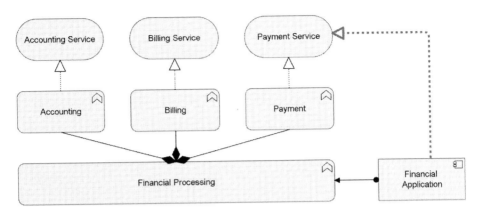

Example 39: Derivation from a Chain of Structural Relationships

B.2.3   Valid Derivations for Dependency Relationships

Part of the language definition is an abstraction rule that states that a structural relationship, and a dependency relationship that join at an intermediate element under certain conditions, can be combined and replaced by the dependency relationship. This rule is split into two parts for both the source and target side of the dependency.

DR 3: Derivation Between Structural and Dependency Relationships

If two relationships $p(a,b):S$ and $q(b,c):T$ exist, with S being a structural relationship and T being a dependency relationship, then a relationship $r(a,c):T$ can be derived.

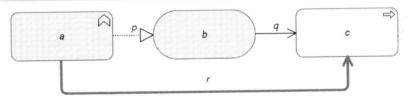

Example 40: Derivation from a Dependency and a Structural Relationship in Line

DR 4: Derivation Between Opposing Structural and Dependency Relationships

If two relationships $p(a,b):S$ and $q(c,b):T$ exist, with S being a structural relationship and T being a dependency relationship, then a relationship $r(c,a):T$ can be derived.

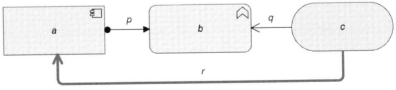

Example 41: Derivation from a Dependency and a Structural Relationship in the Opposite Direction

These rules may be combined with the derivation rule for structural relations (DR2), allowing to replace a "chain" of structural relationships and a dependency relationship (with intermediate model elements) by the dependency relationship in the chain, given that the chain does satisfy the restrictions for structural and dependency relationships. Informally, this means that the begin and/or endpoint of a dependency relationship can be transferred "backwards" in a chain of elements connected by structural relationships.

B.2.4 Valid Derivations for Dynamic Relationships

Part of the language definition is an abstraction rule that states that a structural relationship, and a dynamic relationship that join at an intermediate element under certain conditions, can be combined and replaced by the dynamic relationship. This rule is split into a generic rule and rules specific for flow and triggering.

For the two dynamic relationships, the following rules apply.

DR 5: Derivation Between Structural and Dynamic Relationships

> If two relationships $p(a,b)$:S and $q(b,c)$:T exist, with S being a structural relationship and T being a dynamic relationship, then a relationship $r(a,c)$:T can be derived.

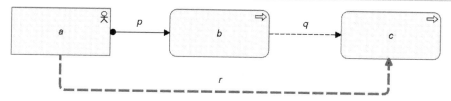

Example 42: Derivation from a Dynamic and a Structural Relationship in Line

DR 6: Derivation Between Structural and Flow Relationships

> If two relationships $p(a,b)$:S and $q(c,b)$:T exist, with S being a structural relationship and T being *Flow*, then a relationship $r(c,a)$:T can be derived.

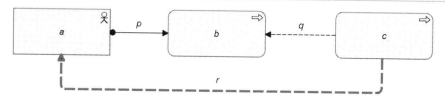

Example 43: Derivation from a Flow and a Structural Relationship in the Opposite Direction

DR 7: Derivation Between Structural and Triggering Relationships

> If two relationships $p(a,b)$:S and $q(b,c)$:T exist, with S being *Triggering* and T being a structural relationship, then a relationships $r(a,c)$:S can be derived.

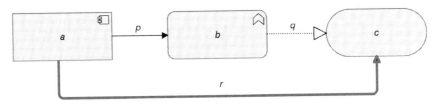

Example 44: Derivation from a Triggering and a Structural Relationship in Line

These rules can be applied repeatedly. Informally, this means that the begin and/or endpoint of a flow relationship can be transferred "backwards" in a chain of elements connected by structural relationships. Example 45 shows two of the possible flow relationships that can be derived with these rules, given a flow relationship between the two services.

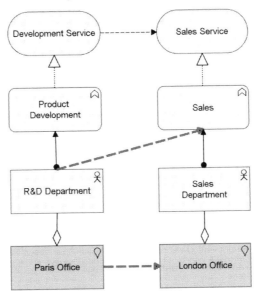

Example 45: Derivation from Dynamic Relationships

Moreover, triggering relationships are *transitive*, as expressed in the next rule.

DR 8: Derivation Between Triggering Relationships

> If two relationships $p(a,b){:}S$ and $q(b,c){:}S$ exist, with S being *Triggering*, then a relationship $r(a,c){:}S$ can be derived.

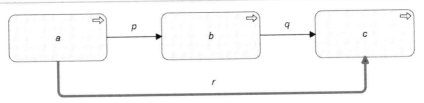

Example 46: Derivation from Triggering Relationships

This rule may be combined with the rules for deriving dynamic relations and structural relationships, thus allowing discovery of triggering relations. Example 47 shows how the "Sales Department" is assigned to a business process "Selling" that triggers a business process "Invoicing", which is composed of the business processes "Billing" and "Payment". "Invoicing" in turn triggers the business process "Shipping", to which the "Shipping Department" is assigned. The derivation rules allow that the "Sales Department" triggers the "Shipping" business process, but also the business process "Billing".

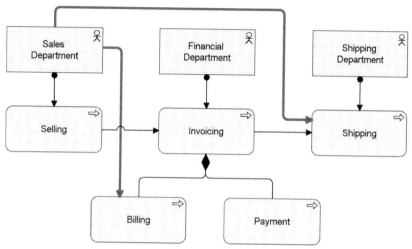

Example 47: Derivation from Triggering and Structural Relationships

B.3   Derivation Rules for Potential Relationships

The derivation rules defined so far lead to relationships that are valid with high certainty. If a model is well designed and describes a stable state of the enterprise, these derived relationships can be trusted.

This section describes derivation rules for relationships with lower certainty. They might be relevant but may also be wrong, depending on the specifics of the model. It is up to the modeler to decide on this.

The derivation rules for potential relationships are used to enrich the metamodel with relationships that otherwise would not be allowed and can be used to discover relationships in a model that otherwise might not show.

Example

Example 48 shows a potential derivation in which some relationships are valuable, and some are not. In this example, an architect first modeled an application component called "Suite" that uses two infrastructure services called "Website Hosting" and "Database Hosting". Later, the application component "Suite" was detailed by adding two composed application components "Front-end" and "Back-end". The architect in this case did not reconsider the serving relations. Potential derivation rule PDR 5 allows the red and grey relationships. In this case, the architect determines that only the red relationships are valuable.

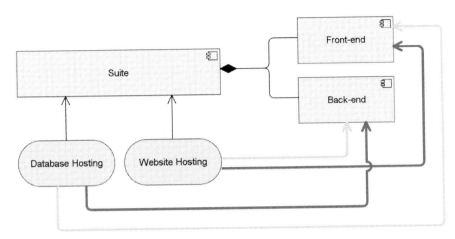

Example 48: Examples of Potential Derivation

B.3.1   Potential Derivation for Specialization Relationships

Part of the language definition is a rule that states that every relation from or to a generic element is inherited by the specialized element. This leads to a number of potential derivations.

The first two rules apply in the case where the target of a specialization relationship is the source or target of any other relationship. In this case, the source of the specialization *could* have the same relationship.

PDR 1: Derivation with Specialization and Other Relationships

If two relationships $p(a,b):S$ and $q(b,c):T$ exist, with S being *Specialization* and T being a structural, dependency, or dynamic relationship, then a relationship $r(a,c):T$ might be derived.

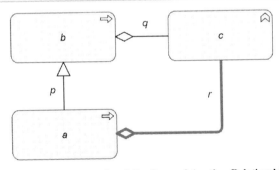

Example 49: Potential Derivation from a Specialization and Another Relationship in Line

PDR 2: Derivation with Specialization and Other Relationships

If two relationships $p(a,b):S$ and $q(c,b):T$ exist, with S being *Specialization* and T being a structural, dependency, or dynamic relationship, then a relationship $r(c,a):T$ might be derived.

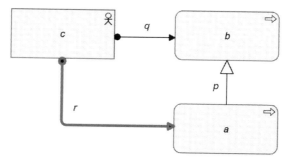

Example 50: Potential Derivation from a Specialization and Another Relationship in the Opposite Direction

The next two rules apply in the case where the source of a specialization relationship is joining the source or target of any other relationship. In this case, the target of the specialization *could* have the same dependency.

PDR 3: Potential Derivation Between Specialization and Any Other Relationship

If two relationships $p(a,b):S$ and $q(a,c):T$ exist, with S being *Specialization* and T being a structural, dependency, or dynamic relationship, then a relation $r(b,c):T$ might be derivable.

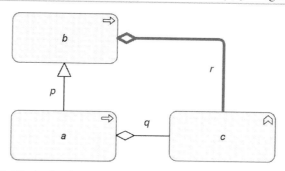

Example 51: Potential Derivation from Another Relationship and a Specialization in Line

PDR 4: Potential Derivation Between Specialization and Any Other Relationship

If two relationships $p(a,b):S$ and $q(c,a):T$ exist, with S being *Specialization* and T being a structural, dependency, or dynamic relationship, then a relationship $r(c,b):T$ might be derivable.

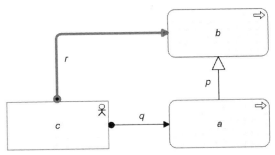

Example 52: Potential Derivation from Another Relationship and a Specialization in Line

The potential relationships derived with the rules from this section may vary a lot in likelihood, depending on the direction of the derivation (from generalized to specialized element or *vice versa*), the type of relationship, and the specific interpretation of the relationship. Also, a chain of multiple potential derivations usually leads to a lower probability.

Consider a model with a "Project Team" assigned to a "Project", and an "IT Project Team", as a specialization of "Project Team", assigned to an I"T Project", as a specialization of "Project". A "Project Team" aggregates a "Project Manager", a "Project" accesses (reads) "Project Planning", and an "IT Project" accesses (writes) "Software Documentation" (Example 53).

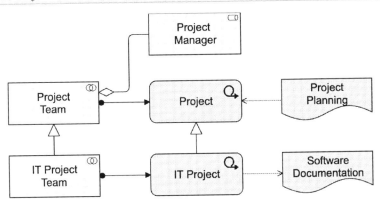

Example 53: Specializations Used in Potential Derivations

- Composition or aggregation relationships often lead to derivations that are (almost) certain when moving the source of the relationship to a specialized element (PDR 1), or the target of the relationship to a generalized element (PDR 4)

  In this example, "IT Project Team" aggregates "Project Manager" is a derived relationship that is almost certain.

- For the assignments, this depends on the perspective: "IT Project Team" assigned to "Project" (PDR 1) is probably true in the sense that the "IT Project Team" always performs a "Project", but uncertain in the sense that a "Project" is not always performed by an "IT Project Team" (e.g., if it is a business project)

  For "Project Team" assigned to "IT Project" (PDR 2), this is the other way around.

- "IT Project" accesses (reads) "Project Planning" (PDR 1) is almost certainly a derived relationship, while "Project" accesses (writes) "Software Documentation" (PDR 3) is only valid for a subset of "Projects"

B.3.2 Potential Derivation for Structural and Dependency Relationships

The next two rules apply in the case where a structural and dependency relation are joining at the source of the structural relation. In this case, the target of the structural relation *could* have the same dependency.

PDR 5: Potential Derivation Between Structural and Dependency Relationships

If two relationships $p(a,b):S$ and $q(c,a):T$ exist, with S being a structural relationship and T being a dependency relationship, then a relationship $r(c,b):T$ might be derivable.

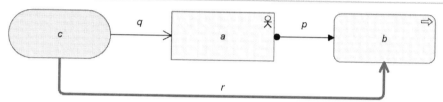

Example 54: Potential Derivation from a Dependency and a Structural Relationship in Line

PDR 6: Potential Derivation Between Structural and Dependency Relationships

If two relationships $p(a,b):S$ and $q(a,c):T$ exist, with S being a structural relationship and T being a dependency relationship, then a relationship $r(b,c):T$ might be derivable.

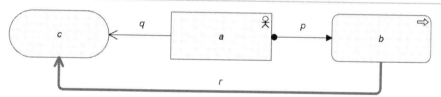

Example 55: Potential Derivation from a Dependency and a Structural Relationship in the Opposite Direction

B.3.3 Potential Derivation for Dependency Relationships

The next rule applies in the case where two dependency relationships are joining at an intermediate element. In this case, the two relations *could* be replaced by one, being the weaker of the two.

The dependency relationships are ordered by "strength":

- Association (weakest)

- Influence

- Access

- Serving (strongest)

The Open Group Standard (2022)

PDR 7: Potential Derivation Between Dependency Relationships

If two relationships $p(a,b)$:S and $q(b,c)$:T exist, with S and T being a *Dependency Relationship*, then a relationship $r(a,c)$:U might be derivable, with U being the weakest of S and T.

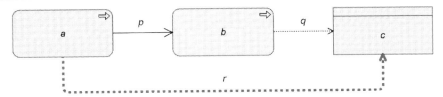

Example 56: Potential Derivation from Two Dependency Relationships

B.3.4   Potential Derivation for Dynamic Relationships

The next rules apply in the case where a structural and dynamic relation are joining at an intermediate element. In this case, the target of the structural relation *could* have the same dependency.

PDR 8: Potential Derivation Between Structural and Dynamic Relationships

If two relationships $p(a,b)$:S and $q(b,c)$:T exist, with S being *Flow* and T being a structural relationship, then a relation $r(a,c)$:S might be derivable.

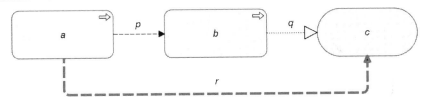

Example 57: Potential Derivation from a Dynamic and a Structural Relationship in Line

PDR 9: Potential Derivation Between Structural and Dynamic Relationships

If two relationships $p(a,b)$:S and $q(a,c)$:T exist, with S being a structural relationship and T being a dynamic relationship, then a relationship $r(b,c)$:T might be derivable.

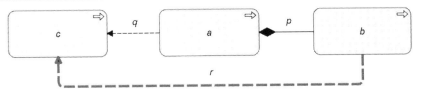

Example 58: Potential Derivation from a Dynamic and a Structural Relationship in the Opposite Direction

The next rule applies in the case where two flow relationships join at an intermediate element. In this case, the flow relations *could* be replaced by one relation.

PDR 10: Potential Derivation Between Flow Relationships

If two relationships $p(a,b):S$ and $q(b,c):S$ exist, with S being *Flow*, then a relationship $r(a,c):S$ might be derivable.

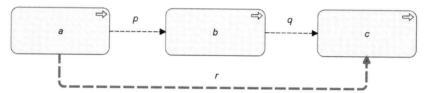

Example 59: Potential Derivation from Two Flow Relationships

PDR 11: Potential Derivation Between Triggering and Structural Relationships

If two relationships $p(a,b):S$ and $q(c,b):T$ exist, with S being a Triggering relationship and T being a structural relationship, then a relation $r(a,c):S$ might be derivable.

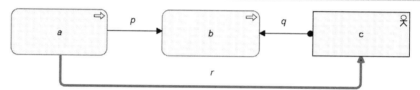

Example 60: Potential Derivation from a Triggering and Structural Relationships

B.3.5   Potential Derivation Rule for Grouping

The next rule applies specifically for the grouping element.

PDR 12: Potential Derivation with Elements Aggregated in a Grouping Element

If two relationships $p(b,a):S$ and $q(b,c):T$ exist, with S being *Aggregation* or *Composition*, b being a Grouping element and T being a *Realization* or *Assignment*, then a relationship $r(a,c):T$ might be derivable, only if the metamodel allows T from a to c.

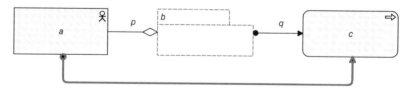

Example 61. Potential Derivation with Grouping Element

B.4   Restrictions on Applying Derivation Rules

This section describes a number of restrictions that apply when using the derivation rules to infer the set of allowed relationships. In this context, the following are called "domains":

- Motivation (Chapter 6)

- Strategy (Chapter 7)

- Core, which includes the Business Layer (Chapter 8), Application Layer (Chapter 9), Technology Layer (Chapter 10), the location element (Section 4.5.2) and the grouping element

- Implementation and Migration (Chapter 12)

Given a relation $p(a,b):S$ that can be derived through one of the derivation rules of Sects. B.2 or B.3, then that derivation is not allowed if any of the following is true:

- a is in one of the domains *Implementation and Migration, Core*, or *Strategy*, and b is in the domain *Motivation*, and S is not *Assignment, Realization, Influence*, or *Association*
- a is in the domain *Motivation*, and b is in one of the domains *Implementation and Migration, Core*, or *Strategy*, and S is not *Association*
- a is in one of the domains *Implementation and Migration* or *Core*, and b is in the domain *Strategy*, and S is not *Realization* or *Association*
- a is in the domain *Strategy*, and b is in one of the domains *Implementation and Migration* or *Core*, and S is not *Association*
- a is in the domain *Implementation and Migration*, and b is in the domain *Core*, and S is not *Realization* or *Association*
- a is in the domain *Core*, and b is in the domain *Implementation and Migration*, and S is not *Assignment* or *Association*
- a is a *Grouping, Location* or *Plateau*, and b is in the domain *Relationships*, and S is not *Composition, Aggregation*, or *Association*
- a is not a *Grouping, Location*, or *Plateau*, and b is in the domain *Relationships*, and S is not *Association*
- a is in the domain *Relationships*, and S is not *Association*
- S is *Influence* and b is not in the domain *Motivation*
- S is *Access* and b is not a *Passive Structure Element*
- a is not a *Passive Structure Element*, and b is a *Passive Structure Element*, and S is not *Access, Assignment*, or *Association*
- a is a *Passive Structure Element*, and b is a *Passive Structure Element*, and S is not *Realization* or *Association*
- a is a *Passive Structure Element*, and b is not a *Passive Structure Element*, and S is not *Realization, Influence*, or *Association*

Given a relation $p(a,b):S$ that can be derived through one of the derivation rules of Sects. B.2 or B.3, with c being the third element on which the original relations joined (for instance $q(a,c):T$ and $r(c,b):U$) than that derivation is not allowed if any of the following is true:

- The domain of c is different from the domains of both a and b, unless a is in domain *Implementation and Migration*, c is in domain *Core*, and b is in one of the domains *Motivation* or *Strategy*

- *a* is in domain *Implementation and Migration*, *b* is in one of the domains *Motivation* or *Strategy*, and *c* is *Location* or *Grouping*

Notes:

- These restrictions only apply to derived relationships, not to relationships explicitly defined in the metamodel diagrams, which are allowed by definition

- Figure 18, which provide the generic structure of layers, are intended as a template for these layers; the subtypes of these elements do not inherit all possible relationships with other subtypes, only with those within their own layer, as specified in the layer-specific metamodel fragments

- Product and plateau are composite elements, but can only aggregate or be composed of the specific concepts depicted in their respective metamodel fragments Figure 68 and Figure 106

B.5 Relationship Tables

This section provides a set of tables with all allowed relationships. It is constructed from the metamodel figures in Chapters 3 through 12 and the derivation rules for relationships outlined in Section B.1.

The letters in the tables have the following meaning:

(a)ccess	(c)omposition	(f)low	a(g)gregation	ass(i)gnment	
i(n)fluence	ass(o)ciation	(r)ealization	(s)pecialization	(t)riggering	ser(v)ing

Motivation

From → / ↓ To		Assessment	Constraint	Driver	Goal	Meaning	Outcome	Principle
Motivation	Assessment	sog N o	N o	N o	N o	N o	N o	N o
	Constraint	r	sog N o	sog r	N o		N r	r
	Driver	N o	N o	sog N o	N o	N o	N o	N o
	Goal	r	r N o	r	sog N o	N o	R N o	r
	Meaning	N o	N o	N o	N o	sog N o	N o	N o
	Outcome	r	R N o	r	N o	r	sog N o	r
	Principle	N o	R N o	N o	N o	N o	N o	sog N o
	Requirement	r	sog N o		N o		N o	r
	Stakeholder	N o	N o	N o	R N o	R N o	N o	N o
	Value	r	N o	r	N o	r	N o	r
Strategy	Capability	o	o	o	o	o	o	o
	Value Stream		o		o		o	
	Course of Action	o	o	o	o	o	o	o
	Resource		o		o		o	
Business	Business Actor	o	o	o	o	o	o	o
	Business Collaboration		o		o		o	
	Business Event		o		o		o	
	Business Function		o		o		o	
	Business Interaction	o	o	o	o	o	o	o
	Business Interface		o		o		o	
	Business Object	o	o	o	o	o	o	o
	Business Process		o		o		o	
	Business Role	o	o	o	o	o	o	o
	Business Service		o		o		o	
	Contract	o	o	o	o	o	o	o
	Product		o		o		o	
	Representation	o	o	o	o	o	o	o
Application	Application Collaboration		o		o		o	
	Application Component	o	o	o	o	o	o	o
	Application Event		o		o		o	
	Application Function	o	o	o	o	o	o	o
	Application Interaction		o		o		o	
	Application Interface	o	o	o	o	o	o	o
	Application Process		o		o		o	
	Application Service	o	o	o	o	o	o	o
	Data Object		o		o		o	
Technology	Artifact	o	o	o	o	o	o	o
	Communication Network		o		o		o	
	Device	o	o	o	o	o	o	o
	Node		o		o		o	
	Path	o	o	o	o	o	o	o
	System Software		o		o		o	
	Technology Collaboration	o	o	o	o	o	o	o
	Technology Event		o		o		o	
	Technology Function	o	o	o	o	o	o	o
	Technology Interaction		o		o		o	
	Technology Interface	o	o	o	o	o	o	o
	Technology Process		o		o		o	
	Technology Service	o	o	o	o	o	o	o
Physical	Distribution Network		o		o		o	
	Equipment	o	o	o	o	o	o	o
	Facility		o		o		o	
	Material	o	o	o	o	o	o	o
Implementation & Migration	Deliverable		o		o		o	
	Implementation Event	o	o	o	o	o	o	o
	Work Package		o		o		o	
	Gap	o	o	o	o	o	o	o
	Plateau		o		o		o	
Other	Location	o	o	o	o	o	o	o
	Grouping	sog r	sog r n o	r	sog n o	r	sog r n o	sog r
		Assessment	Constraint	Driver	Goal	Meaning	Outcome	Principle

From → / ↓ To	Motivation			Strategy			
	Requirement	Stakeholder	Value	Capability	Value Stream	Course of Action	Resource
Motivation							
Assessment	N O	N O	N O	n O	n O	n O	n O
Constraint	SCG N O	N O	N O	R N O	R N O	R N O	R N O
Driver	N O	N O	N O	n O	n O	n O	n O
Goal	r N O	N O	N O	r n O	r n O	r n O	r n O
Meaning	N O	N O	N O	n O	n O	n O	n O
Outcome	R N O	N O	N O	r n O	r n O	R N O	r n O
Principle	R N O	N O	N O	r n O	r n O	r n O	r n O
Requirement	SCG N O	N O	N O	R N O	R N O	R N O	R N O
Stakeholder	N O	SCG N O	N O	n O	n O	n O	n O
Value	N O	N O	SCG N O	n O	n O	n O	n O
Strategy							
Capability	O	O	O	SCG V TFO	V TFO	v tfo	I v tfo
Value Stream	O	O	O	V TFO	SCG V TFO	v tfo	I v tfo
Course of Action	O	O	O	RV tfo	RV tfo	SCG V TFO	rv tfo
Resource	O	O	O	v tfo	v tfo	v tfo	SCG v tfo
Business							
Business Actor	O	O	O	O	O	O	O
Business Collaboration	O	O	O	O	O	O	O
Business Event	O	O	O	O	O	O	O
Business Function	O	O	O	O	O	O	O
Business Interaction	O	O	O	O	O	O	O
Business Interface	O	O	O	O	O	O	O
Business Object	O	O	O	O	O	O	O
Business Process	O	O	O	O	O	O	O
Business Role	O	O	O	O	O	O	O
Business Service	O	O	O	O	O	O	O
Contract	O	O	O	O	O	O	O
Product	O	O	O	O	O	O	O
Representation	O	O	O	O	O	O	O
Application							
Application Collaboration	O	O	O	O	O	O	O
Application Component	O	O	O	O	O	O	O
Application Event	O	O	O	O	O	O	O
Application Function	O	O	O	O	O	O	O
Application Interaction	O	O	O	O	O	O	O
Application Interface	O	O	O	O	O	O	O
Application Process	O	O	O	O	O	O	O
Application Service	O	O	O	O	O	O	O
Data Object	O	O	O	O	O	O	O
Technology							
Artifact	O	O	O	O	O	O	O
Communication Network	O	O	O	O	O	O	O
Device	O	O	O	O	O	O	O
Node	O	O	O	O	O	O	O
Path	O	O	O	O	O	O	O
System Software	O	O	O	O	O	O	O
Technology Collaboration	O	O	O	O	O	O	O
Technology Event	O	O	O	O	O	O	O
Technology Function	O	O	O	O	O	O	O
Technology Interaction	O	O	O	O	O	O	O
Technology Interface	O	O	O	O	O	O	O
Technology Process	O	O	O	O	O	O	O
Technology Service	O	O	O	O	O	O	O
Physical							
Distribution Network	O	O	O	O	O	O	O
Equipment	O	O	O	O	O	O	O
Facility	O	O	O	O	O	O	O
Material	O	O	O	O	O	O	O
Implementation & Migration							
Deliverable	O	O	O	O	O	O	O
Implementation Event	O	O	O	O	O	O	O
Work Package	O	O	O	O	O	O	O
Gap	O	O	O	O	O	O	O
Plateau	O	O	O	O	O	O	O
Other							
Location	O	O	O	O	O	O	O
Grouping	scg r n O	scg n O	scg n O	scg rv ntfo	scg rv ntfo	scg rv ntfo	scgirv ntfo
	Requirement	Stakeholder	Value	Capability	Value Stream	Course of Action	Resource

	From → ↓ To	Business						
		Business Actor	Business Collaboration	Business Event	Business Function	Business Interaction	Business Interface	Business Object
Motivation	Assessment	n o	n o	n o	n o	n o	n o	n o
	Constraint	R N O	R N O	R N O	R N O	R N O	R N O	R N O
	Driver	n o	n o	n o	n o	n o	n o	n o
	Goal	r n o	r n o	r n o	r n o	r n o	r n o	r n o
	Meaning	n o	n o	n o	n o	n o	n o	n o
	Outcome	r n o	r n o	r n o	r n o	r n o	r n o	r n o
	Principle	r n o	r n o	r n o	r n o	r n o	r n o	r n o
	Requirement	R N O	R N O	R N O	R N O	R N O	R N O	R N O
	Stakeholder	I n o	I n o	n o	n o	n o	n o	n o
	Value	n o	n o	n o	n o	n o	n o	n o
Strategy	Capability	r o	r o	o	R o	R o	r o	r o
	Value Stream	r o	r o	o	R o	R o	r o	r o
	Course of Action	r o	r o	o	r o	r o	r o	r o
	Resource	R o	R o	o	o	o	R o	R o
Business	Business Actor	SCG v tfo	G v tfo	v tfo	v tfo	v tfo	V tfo	o
	Business Collaboration	v tfo	SCG v tfo	v tfo	v tfo	v tfo	V tfo	o
	Business Event	I v tfo	I v tfo	SCG v tfo	v TFO	v TFO	v tfo	o
	Business Function	I v tfo	I v tfo	v TFO	SCG v TFO	CG v TFO	v tfo	o
	Business Interaction	I v tfo	I v tfo	v TFO	CG v TFO	SCG v TFO	v tfo	o
	Business Interface	Cgi v tfo	Cgi v tfo	v tfo	v tfo	v tfo	SCG v tfo	o
	Business Object	a o	a o	A o	A o	A o	a o	SCG o
	Business Process	I v tfo	I v tfo	v TFO	CG v TFO	CG v TFO	v tfo	o
	Business Role	I v tfo	Gi v tfo	v tfo	v tfo	v tfo	I v tfo	o
	Business Service	irv tfo	irv tfo	v TFO	Rv tfo	Rv tfo	I v tfo	o
	Contract	a o	a o	A o	A o	A o	a o	SCG o
	Product	v tfo	v tfo	v tfo	v tfo	v tfo	v tfo	o
	Representation	a o	a o	A o	A o	A o	a o	o
Application	Application Collaboration	v tfo	v tfo	v tfo	v tfo	v tfo	V tfo	o
	Application Component	v tfo	v tfo	v tfo	v tfo	v tfo	V tfo	o
	Application Event	v tfo	v tfo	v tfo	v tfo	v tfo	V tfo	o
	Application Function	v tfo	v tfo	v tfo	v tfo	v tfo	V tfo	o
	Application Interaction	v tfo	v tfo	v tfo	v tfo	v tfo	v tfo	o
	Application Interface	v tfo	v tfo	v tfo	v tfo	v tfo	V tfo	o
	Application Process	v tfo	v tfo	v tfo	v tfo	v tfo	V tfo	o
	Application Service	v tfo	v tfo	v tfo	v tfo	v tfo	V tfo	o
	Data Object	a o	a o	a o	a o	a o	a o	o
	Artifact	a o	a o	a o	a o	a o	a o	o
Technology	Communication Network	v tfo	v tfo	v tfo	v tfo	v tfo	V tfo	o
	Device	v tfo	v tfo	v tfo	v tfo	v tfo	V tfo	o
	Node	v tfo	v tfo	v tfo	v tfo	v tfo	V tfo	o
	Path	v tfo	v tfo	v tfo	v tfo	v tfo	V tfo	o
	System Software	v tfo	v tfo	v tfo	v tfo	v tfo	V tfo	o
	Technology Collaboration	v tfo	v tfo	v tfo	v tfo	v tfo	V tfo	o
	Technology Event	v tfo	v tfo	v tfo	v tfo	v tfo	V tfo	o
	Technology Function	v tfo	v tfo	v tfo	v tfo	v tfo	V tfo	o
	Technology Interaction	v tfo	v tfo	v tfo	v tfo	v tfo	v tfo	o
	Technology Interface	v tfo	v tfo	v tfo	v tfo	v tfo	V tfo	o
	Technology Process	v tfo	v tfo	v tfo	v tfo	v tfo	V tfo	o
	Technology Service	v tfo	v tfo	v tfo	v tfo	v tfo	V tfo	o
Physical	Distribution Network	v tfo	v tfo	v tfo	v tfo	v tfo	V tfo	o
	Equipment	v tfo	v tfo	v tfo	v tfo	v tfo	V tfo	o
	Facility	v tfo	v tfo	v tfo	v tfo	v tfo	V tfo	o
	Material	a o	a o	a o	a o	a o	a o	o
Implementation & Migration	Deliverable	o	o	o	o	o	o	o
	Implementation Event	I o	I o	o	o	o	o	o
	Work Package	I o	I o	o	o	o	o	o
	Gap	o	o	o	o	o	o	o
	Plateau	o	o	o	o	o	o	o
Other	Location	v tfo	v tfo	v tfo	v tfo	v tfo	v tfo	o
	Grouping	scgirvantfo	scgirvantfo	scg rvantfo	scgirvantfo	scg rvantfo	scgirvantfo	scg r n o
		Business Actor	Business Collaboration	Business Event	Business Function	Business Interaction	Business Interface	Business Object

		Business					
	From → ↓ To	Business Process	Business Role	Business Service	Contract	Product	Representation
Motivation	Assessment	n O	n O	n O	n O	n O	n O
	Constraint	R N O	R N O	R N O	R N O	R N O	R N O
	Driver	n O	n O			n O	n O
	Goal	r n O	r n O	r n O	r n O	r n O	r n O
	Meaning	n O	n O	n O	n O	n O	n O
	Outcome	r n O	r n O	r n O	r n O	r n O	r n O
	Principle	r n O	r n O	r n O	r n O	r n O	r n O
	Requirement	R N O	R N O	R N O	R N O	R N O	R N O
	Stakeholder	n O	I n O	n O	n O	n O	n O
	Value	n O	n O	n O	n O	n O	n O
Strategy	Capability	R O	r O	R O	r O	r O	r O
	Value Stream	R O	r O	R O	r O	r O	r O
	Course of Action	r O	r O	r O	r O	r O	r O
	Resource	O	R O	O	R O	R O	R O
Business	Business Actor	v tfO	v tfO	V tfO	O	v tfO	O
	Business Collaboration	v tfO	v tfO	V tfO	O	v tfO	O
	Business Event	v TFO	I v tfO	v TFO	O	rv tfO	O
	Business Function	CG v TPO	I v tfO	V tfO	O	rv tfO	O
	Business Interaction	CG v TPO	I v tfO	V tfO	O	rv tfO	O
	Business Interface	v tfO	Cg v tfO	v tfO	O	rv tfO	O
	Business Object	A O	a O	A O	SCG	CG a O	R O
	Business Process	SCG v TPO	I v tfO	V tfO	O	rv tfO	O
	Business Role	v tfO	SCG v tfO	v tfO	O	v tfO	O
	Business Service	Rv tfO	irv tfO	SCG v TFO	O	CG rv tfO	O
	Contract	A O	a O	A O	SCG	CG a O	R O
	Product	v tfO	v tfO	v tfO	O	SCG v tfO	O
	Representation	A O	a O	A O	O	CG a O	SCG O
Application	Application Collaboration	v tfO	v tfO	V tfO	O	rv tfO	O
	Application Component	v tfO	v tfO	V tfO	O	rv tfO	O
	Application Event	v tfO	v tfO	v tfO	O	rv tfO	O
	Application Function	v tfO	v tfO	V tfO	O	rv tfO	O
	Application Interaction	v tfO	v tfO	V tfO	O	rv tfO	O
	Application Interface	v tfO	v tfO	v tfO	O	rv tfO	O
	Application Process	v tfO	v tfO	V tfO	O	rv tfO	O
	Application Service	v tfO	v tfO	v tfO	O	CG rv tfO	O
Technology	Data Object	a O	a O	a O	O	CG a O	O
	Artifact	a O	a O	a O	O	CG a O	O
	Communication Network	v tfO	v tfO	v tfO	O	v tfO	O
	Device	v tfO	v tfO	V tfO	O	rv tfO	O
	Node	v tfO	v tfO	V tfO	O	v tfO	O
	Path	v tfO	v tfO	V tfO	O	v tfO	O
	System Software	v tfO	v tfO	v tfO	O	rv tfO	O
	Technology Collaboration	v tfO	v tfO	v tfO	O	v tfO	O
	Technology Event	v tfO	v tfO	v tfO	O	rv tfO	O
	Technology Function	v tfO	v tfO	v tfO	O	rv tfO	O
	Technology Interaction	v tfO	v tfO	v tfO	O	rv tfO	O
	Technology Interface	v tfO	v tfO	v tfO	O	rv tfO	O
	Technology Process	v tfO	v tfO	V tfO	O	rv tfO	O
	Technology Service	v tfO	v tfO	v tfO	O	CG rv tfO	O
Physical	Distribution Network	v tfO	v tfO	v tfO	O	v tfO	O
	Equipment	v tfO	v tfO	V tfO	O	rv tfO	O
	Facility	v tfO	v tfO	V tfO	O	v tfO	O
	Material	a O	a O	a O	O	CG a O	O
Implementation & Migration	Deliverable	O	O	O	O	O	O
	Implementation Event	O	I O	O	O	O	O
	Work Package	O	I O	O	O	O	O
	Gap	O	O	O	O	O	O
	Plateau	O	O	O	O	O	O
Other	Location	v tfO	v tfO	v tfO	O	v tfO	O
	Grouping	scg rvantfO	scgirvantfO	scg rvantfO	scg r n O	scg rvantfO	scg r n O
		Business Process	Business Role	Business Service	Contract	Product	Representation

	From → ↓ To	Application Collaboration	Application Component	Application Event	Application Function	Application Interaction
Motivation	Assessment	n o	n o	n o	n o	n o
	Constraint	R N o	R N o	R N o	R N o	R N o
	Driver	n o	n o	n o	n o	n o
	Goal	r n o	r n o	r n o	r n o	r n o
	Meaning	n o	n o	n o	n o	n o
	Outcome	r n o	r n o	r n o	r n o	r n o
	Principle	r n o	r n o	r n o	r n o	r n o
	Requirement	R N o	R N o	R N o	R N o	R N o
	Stakeholder	n o	n o	n o	n o	n o
	Value	n o	n o	n o	n o	n o
Strategy	Capability	r o	r o	o	R o	R o
	Value Stream	r o	r o	o	R o	R o
	Course of Action	r o	r o	o	r o	r o
	Resource	R o	R o	o	o	o
Business	Business Actor	v tfo	v tfo	v tfo	v tfo	v tfo
	Business Collaboration	v tfo	v tfo	v tfo	v tfo	v tfo
	Business Event	rv tfo	rv tfo	Rv tfo	v tfo	v tfo
	Business Function	rv tfo	rv tfo	v tfo	Rv tfo	Rv tfo
	Business Interaction	rv tfo	rv tfo	v tfo	Rv tfo	Rv tfo
	Business Interface	rv tfo	rv tfo	v tfo	v tfo	v tfo
	Business Object	a o	a o	a o	a o	a o
	Business Process	rv tfo	rv tfo	v tfo	Rv tfo	Rv tfo
	Business Role	v tfo	v tfo	v tfo	v tfo	v tfo
	Business Service	rv tfo	rv tfo	v tfo	rv tfo	rv tfo
	Contract	a o	a o	a o	a o	a o
	Product	v tfo	v tfo	v tfo	v tfo	v tfo
	Representation	a o	a o	a o	a o	a o
Application	Application Collaboration	SCG v tfo	G rv tfo	v tfo	v tfo	v tfo
	Application Component	G rv tfo	SCG Rv tfo	v tfo	v tfo	v tfo
	Application Event	Irv tfo	Irv tfo	SCG v TFO	v TFO	v TFO
	Application Function	Irv tfo	Irv tfo	v TFO	SCG v TFO	CG v TFO
	Application Interaction	Irv tfo	Irv tfo	v TFO	CG v TFO	SCG v TFO
	Application Interface	Cg rv tfo	Cg rv tfo	v tfo	v tfo	v tfo
	Application Process	Irv tfo	Irv tfo	v TFO	CG v TFO	CG v tfo
	Application Service	irv tfo	irv tfo	v TFO	Rv tfo	Rv tfo
	Data Object	a o	a o	A o	A o	A o
Technology	Artifact	a o	a o	a o	a o	a o
	Communication Network	v tfo	v tfo	v tfo	v tfo	v tfo
	Device	v tfo	v tfo	v tfo	v tfo	v tfo
	Node	v tfo	v tfo	v tfo	v tfo	v tfo
	Path	v tfo	v tfo	v tfo	v tfo	v tfo
	System Software	v tfo	v tfo	v tfo	v tfo	v tfo
	Technology Collaboration	v tfo	v tfo	v tfo	v tfo	v tfo
	Technology Event	v tfo	v tfo	v tfo	v tfo	v tfo
	Technology Function	v tfo	v tfo	v tfo	v tfo	v tfo
	Technology Interaction	v tfo	v tfo	v tfo	v tfo	v tfo
	Technology Interface	v tfo	v tfo	v tfo	v tfo	v tfo
	Technology Process	v tfo	v tfo	v tfo	v tfo	v tfo
	Technology Service	v tfo	v tfo	v tfo	v tfo	v tfo
Physical	Distribution Network	v tfo	v tfo	v tfo	v tfo	v tfo
	Equipment	v tfo	v tfo	v tfo	v tfo	v tfo
	Facility	v tfo	v tfo	v tfo	v tfo	v tfo
	Material	a o	a o	a o	a o	a o
Implementation & Migration	Deliverable	o	o	o	o	o
	Implementation Event	o	o	o	o	o
	Work Package	o	o	o	o	o
	Gap	o	o	o	o	o
	Plateau	o	o	o	o	o
Other	Location	v tfo	v tfo	v tfo	v tfo	v tfo
	Grouping	scgirvantfo	scgirvantfo	scg rvantfo	scg rvantfo	scg rvantfo
		Application Collaboration	Application Component	Application Event	Application Function	Application Interaction

		Application			
	From → ↓ To	Application Interface	Application Process	Application Service	Data Object
Motivation	Assessment	n o	n o	n o	n o
	Constraint	R N O	R N O	R N O	R N O
	Driver	n o	n o	n o	n o
	Goal	r n o	r n o	r n o	r n o
	Meaning	n o	n o	n o	n o
	Outcome	r n o	r n o	r n o	r n o
	Principle	r n o	r n o	r n o	r n o
	Requirement	R N O	R N O	R N O	R N O
	Stakeholder	n o	n o	n o	n o
	Value	n o	n o	n o	n o
Strategy	Capability	r o	R o	R o	r o
	Value Stream	r o	R o	R o	r o
	Course of Action	r o	r o	r o	r o
	Resource	R o	o	o	R o
Business	Business Actor	V tfo	v tfo	V tfo	o
	Business Collaboration	V tfo	v tfo	V tfo	o
	Business Event	V tfo	v tfo	V tfo	o
	Business Function	v tfo	Rv tfo	V tfo	o
	Business Interaction	v tfo	Rv tfo	V tfo	o
	Business Interface	Rv tfo	v tfo	v tfo	o
	Business Object	a o	a o	a o	R o
	Business Process	v tfo	Rv tfo	V tfo	o
	Business Role	V tfo	v tfo	V tfo	o
	Business Service	rv tfo	rv tfo	Rv tfo	o
	Contract	a o	a o	a o	R o
	Product	v tfo	v tfo	v tfo	o
	Representation	a o	a o	a o	o
Application	Application Collaboration	V tfo	v tfo	V tfo	o
	Application Component	V tfo	v tfo	V tfo	o
	Application Event	v tfo	v TFO	v TFO	o
	Application Function	v tfo	CG v TFO	V tfo	o
	Application Interaction	v tfo	CG v TFO	V tfo	o
	Application Interface	SCG v tfo	v tfo	v tfo	o
	Application Process	v tfo	SCG v TFO	V tfo	o
	Application Service	I v tfo	Rv tfo	SCG v TFO	o
	Data Object	a o	A o	A o	SCG o
	Artifact	a o	a o	a o	o
Technology	Communication Network	v tfo	v tfo	v tfo	o
	Device	V tfo	v tfo	V tfo	o
	Node	V tfo	v tfo	V tfo	o
	Path	v tfo	v tfo	v tfo	o
	System Software	V tfo	v tfo	V tfo	o
	Technology Collaboration	V tfo	v tfo	V tfo	o
	Technology Event	v tfo	v tfo	v tfo	o
	Technology Function	v tfo	v tfo	v tfo	o
	Technology Interaction	v tfo	v tfo	V tfo	o
	Technology Interface	v tfo	v tfo	v tfo	o
	Technology Process	v tfo	v tfo	v tfo	o
	Technology Service	v tfo	v tfo	v tfo	o
Physical	Distribution Network	v tfo	v tfo	v tfo	o
	Equipment	V tfo	v tfo	V tfo	o
	Facility	V tfo	v tfo	V tfo	o
	Material	a o	a o	a o	o
Implementation & Migration	Deliverable	o	o	o	o
	Implementation Event	o	o	o	o
	Work Package	o	o	o	o
	Gap	o	o	o	o
	Plateau	o	o	o	o
Other	Location	v tfo	v tfo	v tfo	o
	Grouping	scgirvantfo	scg rvantfo	scg rvantfo	scg r n o
		Application Interface	Application Process	Application Service	Data Object

From → / To ↓		Artifact	Communication Network	Device	Node	Path	System Software	Technology Collaboration
Motivation	Assessment	n o	n o	n o	n o	n o	n o	n o
	Constraint	R N o	R N O	R N o	R N o	R N o	R N O	R N o
	Driver	n o	n o	n o	n o	n o	n o	n o
	Goal	r n o	r n o	r n o	r n o	r n o	r n o	r n o
	Meaning	n o	n o	n o	n o	n o	n o	n o
	Outcome	r n o	r n o	r n o	r n o	r n o	r n o	r n o
	Principle	r n o	r n o	r n o	r n o	r n o	r n o	r n o
	Requirement	R N o	R N o	R N o	R N o	R N o	R N o	R N o
	Stakeholder	n o	r n o	n o	i n o	i n o	n o	n o
	Value	n o	n o	n o	n o	n o	n o	n o
Strategy	Capability	r o	r o	r o	r o	r o	r o	r o
	Value Stream	r o	r o	r o	r o	r o	r o	r o
	Course of Action	r o	r o	r o	r o	r o	r o	r o
	Resource	R o	R o	R o	R o	R o	R o	R o
Business	Business Actor	o	rv tfo	v tfo	i v tfo	i v tfo	v tfo	i v tfo
	Business Collaboration	o	rv tfo	v tfo	i v tfo	i v tfo	v tfo	i v tfo
	Business Event	r o	rv tfo	rv tfo	irv tfo	irv tfo	rv tfo	irv tfo
	Business Function	r o	rv tfo	rv tfo	irv tfo	irv tfo	rv tfo	irv tfo
	Business Interaction	r o	rv tfo	rv tfo	irv tfo	irv tfo	rv tfo	irv tfo
	Business Interface	r o	rv tfo	rv tfo	irv tfo	irv tfo	rv tfo	irv tfo
	Business Object	R o	a o	a o	a o	a o	a o	a o
	Business Process	r o	rv tfo	rv tfo	irv tfo	irv tfo	rv tfo	irv tfo
	Business Role	o	rv tfo	rv tfo	i v tfo	i v tfo	v tfo	i v tfo
	Business Service	r o	rv tfo	rv tfo	irv tfo	irv tfo	rv tfo	irv tfo
	Contract	R o	a o	a o	a o	a o	a o	a o
	Product	o	v tfo	v tfo	v tfo	v tfo	v tfo	v tfo
	Representation	o	a o	a o	a o	a o	a o	a o
Application	Application Collaboration	R o	rv tfo	rv tfo	rv tfo	rv tfo	rv tfo	rv tfo
	Application Component	R o	rv tfo	rv tfo	rv tfo	rv tfo	rv tfo	rv tfo
	Application Event	r o	rv tfo	rv tfo	rv tfo	rv tfo	rv tfo	rv tfo
	Application Function	r o	rv tfo	rv tfo	rv tfo	rv tfo	rv tfo	rv tfo
	Application Interaction	r o	rv tfo	rv tfo	rv tfo	rv tfo	rv tfo	rv tfo
	Application Interface	r o	rv tfo	rv tfo	rv tfo	rv tfo	rv tfo	rv tfo
	Application Process	r o	rv tfo	rv tfo	rv tfo	rv tfo	rv tfo	rv tfo
	Application Service	r o	rv tfo	rv tfo	rv tfo	rv tfo	rv tfo	rv tfo
	Data Object	R o	a o	a o	a o	a o	a o	a o
Technology	Artifact	SCG r o	i a o	I a o	i a o	i a o	I a o	i a o
	Communication Network	o	SCG v tfo	v tfo	v tfo	v tfo	v tfo	v tfo
	Device	o	G rv tfo	SCG v tfo	CGirv tfo	Girv tfo	v tfo	Girv tfo
	Node	o	rv tfo	v tfo	SCGi v tfo	Gi v tfo	v tfo	Gi v tfo
	Path	o	Rv tfo	v tfo	v tfo	SCG v tfo	v tfo	v tfo
	System Software	R	Girv tfo	CGirv tfo	CGirv tfo	Girv tfo	SCGirv tfo	Girv tfo
	Technology Collaboration	o	rv tfo	v tfo	G v tfo	v tfo	v tfo	SCG v tfo
	Technology Event	r o	irv tfo	Irv tfo	Irv tfo	irv tfo	Irv tfo	Irv tfo
	Technology Function	r o	irv tfo	Irv tfo	Irv tfo	irv tfo	Irv tfo	Irv tfo
	Technology Interaction	r o	irv tfo	Irv tfo	Irv tfo	irv tfo	Irv tfo	Irv tfo
	Technology Interface	r o	girv tfo	Cgirv tfo	Cgirv tfo	girv tfo	Cgirv tfo	Cgirv tfo
	Technology Process	r o	irv tfo	Irv tfo	Irv tfo	irv tfo	Irv tfo	Irv tfo
	Technology Service	r o	irv tfo	irv tfo	irv tfo	irv tfo	irv tfo	irv tfo
Physical	Distribution Network	o	v tfo	v tfo	v tfo	v tfo	v tfo	v tfo
	Equipment	o	rv tfo	v tfo	CGirv tfo	Girv tfo	v tfo	Girv tfo
	Facility	o	rv tfo	v tfo	CGi v tfo	Gi v tfo	v tfo	Gi v tfo
	Material	o	a o	a o	i a o	i a o	a o	i a o
Implementation & Migration	Deliverable	o	o	o	o	o	o	o
	Implementation Event	o	o	o	i o	i o	o	i o
	Work Package	o	o	o	i o	i o	o	i o
	Gap	o	o	o	o	o	o	o
	Plateau	o	o	o	o	o	o	o
Other	Location	o	v tfo	v tfo	v tfo	v tfo	v tfo	v tfo
	Grouping	scg r n o	scgirvantfo	scgirvantfo	scgirvantfo	scgirvantfo	scgirvantfo	scgirvantfo
		Artifact	Communication Network	Device	Node	Path	System Software	Technology Collaboration

	From → / ↓ To	Technology					
		Technology Event	Technology Function	Technology Interaction	Technology Interface	Technology Process	Technology Service
Motivation	Assessment	n o	n o	n o	n o	n o	n o
	Constraint	R N O	R N O	R N O	R N O	R N O	R N O
	Driver	n o	n o	n o	n o	n o	n o
	Goal	r n o	r n o	r n o	r n o	r n o	r n o
	Meaning	n o	n o	n o	n o	n o	n o
	Outcome	r n o	r n o	r n o	r n o	r n o	r n o
	Principle	r n o	r n o	r n o	r n o	r n o	r n o
	Requirement	R N O	R N O	R N O	R N O	R N O	R N O
	Stakeholder	n o	n o	n o	n o	n o	n o
	Value	n o	n o	n o	n o	n o	n o
Strategy	Capability	O	R O	P O	r O	R O	R O
	Value Stream	O	R O	R O	r O	R O	R O
	Course of Action	O	r O	r O	r O	r O	r O
	Resource	O	O	O	R O	O	O
Business	Business Actor	v tfo	v tfo	v tfo	V tfo	v tfo	V tfo
	Business Collaboration	v tfo	v tfo	v tfo	V tfo	v tfo	V tfo
	Business Event	Rv tfo	v tfo	v tfo	v tfo	v tfo	v tfo
	Business Function	v tfo	Rv tfo	Rv tfo	v tfo	Rv tfo	V tfo
	Business Interaction	v tfo	Rv tfo	Rv tfo	v tfo	Rv tfo	V tfo
	Business Interface	v tfo	v tfo	v tfo	Rv tfo	v tfo	v tfo
	Business Object	a o	a o	a o	a o	a o	a o
	Business Process	v tfo	Rv tfo	Rv tfo	v tfo	Rv tfo	V tfo
	Business Role	v tfo	v tfo	v tfo	V tfo	v tfo	V tfo
	Business Service	v tfo	rv tfo	rv tfo	rv tfo	rv tfo	Rv tfo
	Contract	a o	a o	a o	a o	a o	a o
	Product	v tfo	v tfo	v tfo	v tfo	v tfo	v tfo
	Representation	a o	a o	a o	a o	a o	a o
Application	Application Collaboration	v tfo	v tfo	v tfo	V tfo	v tfo	V tfo
	Application Component	v tfo	v tfo	v tfo	V tfo	v tfo	V tfo
	Application Event	Rv tfo	v tfo	v tfo	v tfo	v tfo	v tfo
	Application Function	v tfo	Rv tfo	Rv tfo	v tfo	Rv tfo	V tfo
	Application Interaction	v tfo	Rv tfo	Rv tfo	v tfo	Rv tfo	V tfo
	Application Interface	v tfo	v tfo	v tfo	Rv tfo	v tfo	v tfo
	Application Process	v tfo	Rv tfo	Rv tfo	v tfo	Rv tfo	V tfo
	Application Service	v tfo	rv tfo	rv tfo	rv tfo	rv tfo	Rv tfo
	Data Object	a o	a o	a o	a o	a o	a o
Technology	Artifact	A o	A o	A o	a o	A o	A o
	Communication Network	v tfo	v tfo	v tfo	v tfo	v tfo	v tfo
	Device	v tfo	v tfo	v tfo	V tfo	v tfo	V tfo
	Node	v tfo	v tfo	v tfo	v tfo	v tfo	V tfo
	Path	v tfo	v tfo	v tfo	v tfo	v tfo	V tfo
	System Software	v tfo	v tfo	v tfo	V tfo	v tfo	V tfo
	Technology Collaboration	v tfo	v tfo	v tfo	V tfo	v tfo	V tfo
	Technology Event	SCG v TFO	v TFO	v TFO	v tfo	v TFO	v TFO
	Technology Function	v TFO	SCG v TFO	CG v TFO	v tfo	CG v TFO	V tfo
	Technology Interaction	v TFO	CG v TFO	SCG v TFO	v tfo	CG v TFO	V tfo
	Technology Interface	v tfo	v tfo	v tfo	SCG v tfo	v tfo	v tfo
	Technology Process	v TFO	CG v TFO	CG v TFO	v tfo	SCG v TFO	V tfo
	Technology Service	v TFO	Rv tfo	Rv tfo	I v tfo	Rv tfo	SCG v TFO
Physical	Distribution Network	v tfo	v tfo	v tfo	v tfo	v tfo	v tfo
	Equipment	v tfo	v tfo	v tfo	V tfo	v tfo	V tfo
	Facility	v tfo	v tfo	v tfo	V tfo	v tfo	V tfo
	Material	A o	A o	A o	a o	A o	A o
Implementation & Migration	Deliverable	o	o	o	o	o	o
	Implementation Event	o	o	o	o	o	o
	Work Package	o	o	o	o	o	o
	Gap	o	o	o	o	o	o
	Plateau	o	o	o	o	o	o
Other	Location	v tfo	v tfo	v tfo	v tfo	v tfo	v tfo
	Grouping	scg rvantfo	scg rvantfo	scg rvantfo	scgirvantfo	scg rvantfo	scg rvantfo
		Technology Event	Technology Function	Technology Interaction	Technology Interface	Technology Process	Technology Service

		Physical			
	From → ↓ To	Distribution Network	Equipment	Facility	Material
Motivation	Assessment	n O	n O	a O	n O
	Constraint	R N O	R N	R N O	R N
	Driver	n O	n O	n O	
	Goal	r n O	r n O	r n O	r n
	Meaning	n O	n O	n O	n O
	Outcome	r n O	r n	r n O	r n
	Principle	r n O	r n O	r n O	r n O
	Requirement	R N O	R N	R N O	R N
	Stakeholder	i r n O	n O	i n O	n O
	Value	n O	n	n O	n
Strategy	Capability	r O	r O	r O	r O
	Value Stream	r O	r O	r O	
	Course of Action	r O	r O	r O	r
	Resource	R O	R O	R O	R
Business	Business Actor	irv tfO	v tfO	iv tfO	O
	Business Collaboration	irv tfO	tfO	iv tfO	
	Business Event	irv tfO	irv tfO	irv tfO	r O
	Business Function	irv tfO	tfO	irv tfO	
	Business Interaction	irv tfO	rv tfO	irv tfO	r
	Business Interface	irv tfO	rv tfO	irv tfO	
	Business Object	a O	a O	a O	R O
	Business Process	irv tfO	tfO	irv tfO	r
	Business Role	irv tfO	v tfO	iv tfO	O
	Business Service	irv tfO	rv tfO	irv tfO	r
	Contract	a O	a O	a O	R O
	Product	v tfO	tf	v tfO	
	Representation	a O	a O	a O	O
Application	Application Collaboration	rv tfO	r tf	rv tfO	r
	Application Component	rv tfO	rv tfO	rv tfO	r O
	Application Event	rv tfO	rv tfO	rv tfO	r
	Application Function	rv tfO	rv tfO	rv tfO	r O
	Application Interaction	rv tfO	r tf	rv tfO	r
	Application Interface	rv tfO	rv tfO	rv tfO	r O
	Application Process	rv tfO	r tf	rv tfO	r
	Application Service	rv tfO	rv tfO	rv tfO	r
	Data Object	a O	a O	a O	r
Technology	Artifact	i a O	i a O	i a O	r O
	Communication Network	v tfO	tfO	v tfO	
	Device	girv tfO	CG rv tfO	cgirv tfO	r O
	Node	girv tfO	v tf	CGi v tfO	
	Path	Rv tfO	v tfO	v tfO	O
	System Software	girv tfO	cgirv tf	cgirv tfO	r
	Technology Collaboration	rv tfO	tfO	rv tfO	O
	Technology Event	irv tfO	irv tf	irv tfO	r
	Technology Function	irv tfO	irv tfO	irv tfO	r
	Technology Interaction	irv tfO	irv tf	Irv tfO	
	Technology Interface	girv tfO	Cgirv tfO	Cgirv tfO	r
	Technology Process	irv tfO	irv tf	Irv tfO	
	Technology Service	irv tfO	irv tfO	irv tfO	r
Physical	Distribution Network	SCG v tfO	tfO	v tfO	
	Equipment	Girv tfO	SCG rv tfO	CGirv tfO	R
	Facility	Girv tfO	tf	SCGi v tfO	
	Material	i a O	i a O	i a O	SCG r O
Implementation & Migration	Deliverable	O		O	
	Implementation Event	i O	O	i O	
	Work Package	i O	O	i O	
	Gap	O	O	O	O
Other	Plateau	O		O	
	Location	v tfO	v tfO	v tfO	O
	Grouping	acgirvantfO	cgirvantf..	acgirvantfO	acg r n O
		Distribution Network	Equipment	Facility	Material

		Implementation & Migration					Other	
↓ To	**From →**	**Deliverable**	**Implementation Event**	**Work Package**	**Gap**	**Plateau**	**Location**	**Grouping**
Motivation	Assessment	n O	n O	n O	O	n O	CG n O	sCG n O
	Constraint	R N O	n	r n O		CG R N O	CG R N	sCG R N O
	Driver	n O	n O	n O		n O	CG n O	sCG n O
	Goal	r n O	n O	r n O		CG r n O	CGr n	sCG r n O
	Meaning	n O	n O	n O	O	n O	CG n O	sCG n O
	Outcome	r n O	n O	r n O		CG r n O	CG r n O	sCG r n O
	Principle	r n O	n O	r n O	O	r n O	CG r n O	sCG r n O
	Requirement	R N O	n	r n O		CG R N O	CG R N	sCG R N O
	Stakeholder	r n O	n O	r n O		ir n O	CGir n O	saCGir n O
	Value	n O	n O	n O	O	n O	CG n O	sCG n O
Strategy	Capability	R O		R O	O	CG R O	CG r	sCGirv tfO
	Value Stream	R O		R O		CG R	CG r	sCGirv tfO
	Course of Action	R O	O	R O	O	CG R	CG r	sCG rv tfO
	Resource	R O		R O		CG R	CG R	aCG rv tfO
Business	Business Actor	R O		R O	O	CG R	CGirv tfO	sCGirv tfO
	Business Collaboration	R O		R O	O	CG R	CGirv tfO	sCGirv tfO
	Business Event	R O		R O	O	CG R	CGirv tfO	sCGirv tfO
	Business Function	R O		R O		CG R	CGirv tfO	sCGirv tfO
	Business Interaction	R O		R O	O	CG R	CGirv tfO	sCGirv tfO
	Business Interface	R O		R O		CG R	CGirv tfO	sCGirv tfO
	Business Object	R O		R O		CG R	CG a O	sCG r a O
	Business Process	R O		R O		CG R	CGirv tfO	sCGirv tfO
	Business Role	R O		R O		CG R	CGirv tfO	sCGirv tfO
	Business Service	R O		R O		CG R	CGirv tfO	sCGirv tfO
	Contract	R O	O	R O		CG R O	CG a O	sCG r a O
	Product	R O		R O		CG R	CG v O	aCG rv tfO
	Representation	R O		R O		CG R	CG a O	sCG r a O
Application	Application Collaboration	R O		R O		CG R	CG rv tfO	sCG rv tfO
	Application Component	R O	O	R O	O	CG R	CG rv tfO	sCG rv tfO
	Application Event	R O		R O		CG R	CGirv tfO	sCGirv tfO
	Application Function	R O		R O		CG R	CGirv tfO	sCGirv tfO
	Application Interaction	R O		R O		CG R	CGirv tfO	sCGirv tfO
	Application Interface	R O	O	R O		CG R	CG rv tfO	sCG rv tfO
	Application Process	R O		R O		CG R	CGirv tfO	sCGirv tfO
	Application Service	R O		R O		CG R	CGirv tfO	sCGirv tfO
	Data Object	R O		R O		CG R	CG a O	sCG r a O
Technology	Artifact	R O		R O	O	CG R	CGi a O	sCGi a O
	Communication Network	R O		R O		CG R	CG v tfO	sCG rv tfO
	Device	R O	O	R O	O	CG R	CGirv tfO	sCGirv tfO
	Node	R O		R O		CG R	CGirv tfO	sCGirv tfO
	Path	R O	O	R O		CG R	CG v tfO	sCG rv tfO
	System Software	R O		R O		CG R	CGirv tfO	sCGirv tfO
	Technology Collaboration	R O		R O	O	CG R	CGirv tfO	sCG rv tfO
	Technology Event	R O		R O		CG R	CGirv tfO	sCGirv tfO
	Technology Function	R O		R O		CG R	CGirv tfO	sCGirv tfO
	Technology Interaction	R O		R O		CG R	CGirv tfO	sCGirv tfO
	Technology Interface	R O	O	R O		CG R	CGirv tfO	sCGirv tfO
	Technology Process	R O		R O		CG R	CGirv tfO	sCGirv tfO
	Technology Service	R O		R O		CG R	CGirv tfO	sCGirv tfO
Physical	Distribution Network	R O		R O		CG R	CG	sCG rv tfO
	Equipment	R O		R O		CG R	CGirv tfO	sCGirv tfO
	Facility	R O		R O	O	CG R	CGirv tfO	sCGirv tfO
	Material	R O	O	R O	O	CG R	CGi a O	sCGi a O
Implementation & Migration	Deliverable	SCG O	A	R A O		a O	CG	sCG r a O
	Implementation Event	O	SCG TfO	TfO	O	TfO	CGi	sCGi tfO
	Work Package	O	TfO	SCG TfO		tfO	CGi	sCGi tfO
	Gap			O	SCG		CG	sCG O
	Plateau	R O	Tf	r tfO	SCG		SCG r O	sCG r tfO
Other	Location	R O	O	R O	O	CG R O	sCG v tfO	sCG rv tfO
	Grouping	scg r n O	scg	scg r antfO	scg	scgir antfO	sCGirv antfO	sCGirvantfO
		Deliverable	**Implementation Event**	**Work Package**	**Gap**	**Plateau**	**Location**	**Grouping**

B.6 Grouping, Plateau, and Relationships Between Relationships

In addition to the relationships derived using the rules specified in Sections B.2 and B.3, the following relationships are also allowed for grouping, plateau, relationships, and relationship connectors:

- Grouping and location elements may have an aggregation or composition relationship to any concept (element, relationships, or relationship connectors)

- A grouping element may be the source of any relationship with any element (provided that the element is a possible target element for the relationship)

- A grouping element may be the target of any relationship with any element (provided that the element is a possible source element for the relationship)

- A grouping element may have any relationship with another grouping element

- Any relationship may have an association relationship with any element

The resulting relationships between elements have been added to the table in Section B.5 and are summarized in Table 21.

Table 21: Grouping, Plateau, and Relationships Between Relationships

From → ↓ To	Grouping	Plateau/ Location	Element other than Grouping, Plateau, Location	Relationship	Relationship Connector
Grouping	any	cg + any**	any**	o	afinortv*
Element other than Grouping	any*	See metamodel.	See metamodel.	o	afinortv*
Relationship	cg + o	cg + o	o		o
Relationship Connector	afinortv	afinortv**	afinortv**	o	afinortv

* Provided that element is a possible target element of the relationship (see Section B.5).

** Provided that element is a possible source element of the relationship (see Section B.5).

(a)ccess   (c)omposition   (f)low   a(g)gregation   ass(i)gnment
i(n)fluence   ass(o)ciation   (r)ealization   (s)pecialization   (t)riggering   ser(v)ing

C Example Viewpoints

C.1 Basic Viewpoints in the ArchiMate Language

A viewpoint in the ArchiMate language is a selection of a relevant subset of the ArchiMate elements and their relationships. This is the representation of that part of an architecture that is expressed in different diagrams.

A basic type of viewpoint, is a simple selection of a relevant subset of ArchiMate concepts. The expressed representation of that part of an architecture in this section is geared towards the stakeholders that will utilize the resulting views.

The following are examples of stakeholders and concerns as a basis for the specification of viewpoints:

- End user

  For example, what are the consequences for their work and workplace?

- Architect

  What is the consequence for the maintainability of a system, with respect to corrective, preventive, and adaptive maintenance?

- Upper-level management

  How can we ensure our policies are followed in the development and operation of processes and systems? What is the impact of decisions (on personnel, finance, ICT, etc.)?

- Operational Manager

  Responsible for exploitation or maintenance; for example, what new technologies are there to prepare for? Is there a need to adapt maintenance processes? What is the impact of changes to existing applications? How secure are my systems?

- Project Manager

  Responsible for the development of new applications. What are the relevant domains and their relationships? What is the dependence of business processes on the applications to be built? What is their expected performance?

- Developer

  What are the modifications with respect to the current situation that need to be done?

In each basic viewpoint, concepts from the three layers of Business, Application, and Technology may be used. However, not every combination of these would give meaningful results. In some cases, separate viewpoints for the different layers are advisable. Based on common architectural practice and on experiences with the use of ArchiMate models in practical cases, useful combinations in the form of a set of basic viewpoints have been defined. These are listed in Table 22. The table also shows the perspective for the viewpoint. Some viewpoints have a scope that is limited to a single layer or aspect, when others link multiple layers and/or aspects. The different viewpoints are grouped into categories that indicate which direction and which elements the viewpoint is looking at:

1.   *Composition*: viewpoints that define internal compositions and aggregations of elements.

2.   *Support*: viewpoints where you are looking at elements that are supported by other elements, typically from one layer and upwards to an above layer.

3.   *Cooperation*: towards peer elements which cooperate with each other, typically across aspects.

4.   *Realization*: viewpoints where you are looking at elements that realize other elements, typically from one layer and downwards to a below layer.

Table 22: Basic Viewpoints

Category: Composition		
Name	**Perspective**	**Scope**
Organization	Structure of the enterprise in terms of roles, departments, etc.	Single layer, single aspect
Application Structure	Shows the structure of a typical application in terms of its constituents.	Single layer, multiple aspects
Information Structure	Shows the structure of the information used in the enterprise.	Multiple layers, single aspects
Technology	Infrastructure and platforms underlying the enterprise's information systems in terms of networks, devices, and system software.	Single layer, multiple aspects
Layered	Provides overview of architecture(s).	Multiple layers, multiple aspects
Physical	Physical environment and how this relates to IT infrastructure.	Multiple layers, multiple aspects
Category: Support		
Name	**Perspective**	**Scope**
Product	Shows the contents of products.	Multiple layers, multiple aspects
Application Usage	Relates applications to their use in, for example, business processes.	Multiple layers, multiple aspects
Technology Usage	Shows how technology is used by applications.	Multiple layers, multiple aspects
Category: Cooperation		
Name	**Perspective**	**Scope**
Business Process Cooperation	Shows the relationships between various business processes.	Multiple layers, multiple aspects

Application Cooperation	Shows application components and their mutual relationships.	Application layer, multiple aspects
Category: Realization		
Name	**Perspective**	**Scope**
Service Realization	Shows how services are realized by the requisite behavior.	Multiple layers, multiple aspects
Implementation and Deployment	Shows how applications are mapped onto the underlying technology.	Multiple layers, multiple aspects

In the following sections, the ArchiMate viewpoints are described in more detail. For each viewpoint, the comprised elements are listed guidelines for the viewpoint's use, and the stakeholder concerns addressed by the viewpoint are indicated. In addition to the specified elements, the grouping element, junction, and or junction can be used in every viewpoint. For more details on the goal and use of viewpoints, refer to Chapter 14 of [1].

These basic viewpoints are starting points for modeling efforts. They can accelerate architectural efforts, support organizational standards, facilitate peer review, and aid new modelers. However, these basic viewpoints should not constrain modeling activities. Organizations and individual modelers should address stakeholder concerns by selecting from the basic viewpoints, modifying them, or defining new ones. The viewpoints listed here are therefore intended as examples, not as a normative or exhaustive list.

As outlined before, a viewpoint's representation should be geared towards the intended stakeholder(s). This means that these basic viewpoints are mainly useful for architects and their peers. Other stakeholders may require a different representation, even if they are interested in the same content.

C.1.1 Organization Viewpoint

The organization viewpoint focuses on the (internal) organization of a company, department, network of companies, or of another organizational entity. It is possible to present models in this viewpoint as nested block diagrams, but also in a more traditional way, such as organizational charts. The organization viewpoint is very useful in identifying competencies, authority, and responsibilities in an organization.

Table 23: Organization Viewpoint Description

Organization Viewpoint	
Stakeholders	Enterprise, Process and Domain Architects, managers, employees, shareholders
Concerns	Identification of competencies, authority, and responsibilities
Purpose	Designing, deciding, informing
Scope	Single layer/Single aspect

Elements

- Business actor
- Business role
- Business collaboration
- Location
- Business interface

C.1.2   Application Structure Viewpoint

The application structure viewpoint shows the structure of one or more applications or components. This viewpoint is useful in designing or understanding the main structure of applications or components and the associated data; e.g., to break down the structure of the system under construction, or to identify legacy application components that are suitable for migration/integration.

Table 24: Application Structure Viewpoint Description

Application Structure Viewpoint	
Stakeholders	Application and Solution Architects
Concerns	Application structure, consistency and completeness, reduction of complexity
Purpose	Designing
Scope	Single layer/Multiple aspects

Elements

- Application component
- Application interface
- Application collaboration
- Data object

C.1.3   Information Structure Viewpoint

The information structure viewpoint is comparable to the traditional information models created in the development of almost any information system. It shows the structure of the information used in the enterprise or in a specific business process or application, in terms of data types or (object-oriented) class structures. Furthermore, it may show how the information at the business level is represented at the application level in the form of the data structures used there, and how these are then mapped onto the underlying technology infrastructure; e.g., by means of a database schema.

Table 25: Information Structure Viewpoint Description

Information Structure Viewpoint	
Stakeholders	Domain and Information Architects
Concerns	Structure and dependencies of the used data and information, consistency, and completeness
Purpose	Designing
Scope	Multiple layers/Single aspects

Elements

- Business object
- Representation
- Data object
- Artifact
- Meaning

C.1.4   Technology Viewpoint

The technology viewpoint contains the software and hardware technology elements supporting the Application Layer, such as physical devices, networks, or system software (e.g., operating systems, databases, and middleware).

Table 26: Technology Viewpoint Description

Technology Viewpoint	
Stakeholders	Infrastructure Architects, Operational Managers
Concerns	Stability, security, dependencies, costs of the infrastructure
Purpose -	Designing
Scope	Single layer/Multiple aspects

Elements

- Location
- Node
- Technology collaboration
- Device
- System software
- Technology interface
- Communication network
- Path
- Technology process/function/interaction
- Technology service
- Technology event

- Artifact

C.1.5 Layered Viewpoint

The layered viewpoint pictures several layers and aspects of an Enterprise Architecture in one diagram. There are two categories of layers, namely *dedicated layers* and *service layers*. The layers are the result of the use of the "grouping" relationship for a natural partitioning of the entire set of objects and relationships that belong to a model. The technology, application, process, and actor/role layers belong to the first category. The structural principle behind a fully layered viewpoint is that each dedicated layer exposes, by means of the "realization" relationship, a layer of services, which are further on "serving" the next dedicated layer. Thus, we can easily separate the internal structure and organization of a dedicated layer from its externally observable behavior expressed as the service layer that the dedicated layer realizes. The order, number, or nature of these layers are not fixed, but in general a (more or less) complete and natural layering of an ArchiMate model should contain the succession of layers depicted in the example given in Table 27. However, this example is by no means intended to be prescriptive. The main goal of the layered viewpoint is to provide an overview in one diagram. Furthermore, this viewpoint can be used as support for impact of change analysis and performance analysis or for extending the service portfolio.

Table 27: Layered Viewpoint Description

Layered Viewpoint	
Stakeholders	Enterprise, Process, Application, Infrastructure, and Domain Architects
Concerns	Consistency, reduction of complexity, impact of change, flexibility
Purpose	Designing, deciding, informing
Scope	Multiple layers/Multiple aspects

Elements

All core elements and all relationships are permitted in this viewpoint.

C.1.6 Physical Viewpoint

The physical viewpoint contains equipment (one or more physical machines, tools, or instruments) that can create, use, store, move, or transform materials, how the equipment is connected via the distribution network, and what other active elements are assigned to the equipment.

Table 28: Physical Viewpoint Description

Physical Viewpoint	
Stakeholders	Infrastructure Architects, Operational Managers
Concerns	Relationships and dependencies of the physical environment and how this relates to IT infrastructure
Purpose	Designing

Physical Viewpoint	
Scope	Multiple layers/Multiple aspects

Elements

- Location
- Node
- Device
- Equipment
- Facility
- Path
- Communication network
- Distribution network
- Material

C.1.7 Product Viewpoint

The product viewpoint depicts the value that these products offer to the customers or other external parties involved. It shows the composition of one or more products in terms of the constituting (business, application, or technology) services, and the associated contract(s) or other agreements. It may also be used to show the interfaces (channels) through which this product is offered, and the events associated with the product. A product viewpoint is typically used in product development to design a product by composing existing services or by identifying which new services have to be created for this product, given the value a customer expects from it. It may then serve as input for business process architects and others that need to design the processes and ICT realizing these products.

Table 29: Product Viewpoint Description

Product Viewpoint	
Stakeholders	Product Developers, Product Managers, Process and Domain Architects
Concerns	Product development, value offered by the products of the enterprise
Purpose	Designing, deciding
Scope	Multiple layers/Multiple aspects

Elements

- Business actor
- Business role
- Business collaboration
- Business interface
- Business process/function/interaction
- Business event
- Business service
- Business object

- Product
- Contract
- Application component/collaboration
- Application interface
- Application process/function/interaction
- Application event
- Application service
- Data object
- Technology service
- Artifact
- Material
- Value

C.1.8   Application Usage Viewpoint

The application usage viewpoint describes how applications are used to support one or more business processes, and how they are used by other applications. It can be used in designing an application by identifying the services needed by business processes and other applications, or in designing business processes by describing the services that are available. Furthermore, since it identifies the dependencies of business processes upon applications, it may be useful to operational managers responsible for these processes.

Table 30: Application Usage Viewpoint Description

Application Usage Viewpoint	
Stakeholders	Enterprise, Process, and Application Architects, Operational Managers
Concerns	Consistency and completeness, reduction of complexity
Purpose	Designing, deciding
Scope	Multiple layers/Multiple aspects

Elements

- Business actor
- Business role
- Business collaboration
- Business process/function/interaction
- Business event
- Business object
- Application component/collaboration
- Application interface
- Application process/function/interaction
- Application event
- Application service
- Data object

C.1.9 Technology Usage Viewpoint

The technology usage viewpoint shows how applications are supported by the software and hardware technology: the technology services are delivered by the devices; system software and networks are provided to the applications. This viewpoint plays an important role in the analysis of performance and scalability, since it relates the physical infrastructure to the logical world of applications. It is very useful in determining the performance and quality requirements on the infrastructure based on the demands of the various applications that use it.

Table 31: Technology Usage Viewpoint Description

Technology Usage Viewpoint	
Stakeholders	Application, Infrastructure Architects, Operational Managers
Concerns	Dependencies, performance, scalability
Purpose	Designing
Scope	Multiple layers/Multiple aspects

Elements

- Application component/collaboration
- Application process/function/interaction
- Application event
- Data object
- Node
- Device
- Technology collaboration
- System software
- Technology interface
- Communication network
- Path
- Technology process/function/interaction
- Technology service
- Technology event
- Artifact

C.1.10 Business Process Cooperation Viewpoint

The business process cooperation viewpoint is used to show the relationships of one or more business processes with each other and/or with their environment. It can be used both to create a high-level design of business processes within their context and to provide an operational manager responsible for one or more such processes with insight into their dependencies. Important aspects of business process cooperation are:

- Causal relationships between the main business processes of the enterprise

- Mapping of business processes onto business functions

- Realization of services by business processes

- Use of shared data

Each of these can be regarded as a "sub-viewpoint" of the business process cooperation viewpoint.

Table 32: Business Process Cooperation Viewpoint Description

Business Process Cooperation Viewpoint	
Stakeholders	Process and Domain Architects, Operational Managers
Concerns	Dependencies between business processes, consistency and completeness, responsibilities
Purpose	Designing, deciding
Scope	Multiple layers/Multiple aspects

Elements

- Business actor
- Business role
- Business collaboration
- Location
- Business interface
- Business process/function/interaction
- Business event
- Business service
- Business object
- Representation
- Application component/collaboration
- Application interface
- Application process/function/interaction
- Application event
- Application service
- Data object

C.1.11   Application Cooperation Viewpoint

The application cooperation viewpoint describes the relationships between application components in terms of the information flows between them, or in terms of the services they offer and use. This viewpoint is typically used to create an overview of the application landscape of an organization. This viewpoint is also used to express the (internal) cooperation or orchestration of services that together support the execution of a business process.

Table 33: Application Cooperation Viewpoint Description

Application Cooperation Viewpoint	
Stakeholders	Enterprise, Process, Application, and Domain Architects

Application Cooperation Viewpoint	
Concerns	Relationships and dependencies between applications, orchestration/choreography of services, consistency and completeness, reduction of complexity
Purpose	Designing
Scope	Application layer/Multiple aspects

Elements

- Location
- Application component/collaboration
- Application interface
- Application process/function/interaction
- Application event
- Application service
- Data object

C.1.12   Service Realization Viewpoint

The service realization viewpoint is used to show how one or more business services are realized by the underlying processes (and sometimes by application components). Thus, it forms the bridge between the business products viewpoint and the business process view. It provides a "view from the outside" on one or more business processes.

Table 34: Service Realization Viewpoint Description

Service Realization Viewpoint	
Stakeholders	Process and Domain Architects, Product and Operational Managers
Concerns	Added-value of business processes, consistency and completeness, responsibilities
Purpose	Designing, deciding
Scope	Multiple layers/Multiple aspects

Elements

- Business actor
- Business role
- Business collaboration
- Business interface
- Business process/function/interaction
- Business event
- Business service
- Business object
- Representation

- Application component/collaboration
- Application interface
- Application process/function/interaction
- Application event
- Application service
- Data object

C.1.13   Implementation and Deployment Viewpoint

The implementation and deployment viewpoint shows how one or more applications are realized on the infrastructure. This comprises the mapping of applications and components onto artifacts, and the mapping of the information used by these applications and components onto the underlying storage infrastructure.

Table 35: Implementation and Deployment Viewpoint Description

Implementation and Deployment Platform Viewpoint	
Stakeholders	Application and Domain Architects
Concerns	Structure of application platforms and how they relate to supporting technology
Purpose	Designing, deciding
Scope	Multiple layers/Multiple aspects

Elements

- Application component/collaboration
- Application interface
- Application process/function/interaction
- Application event
- Application service
- Data object
- System software
- Technology interface
- Path
- Technology process/function/interaction
- Technology service
- Artifact

C.2   Motivation Viewpoints

A number of standard viewpoints for modeling motivational aspects have been defined. Each of these viewpoints presents a different perspective on modeling the motivation that underlies some Enterprise Architecture and allows a modeler to focus on certain aspects. Therefore, each viewpoint considers only a selection of the elements and relationships that have been described in the preceding sections.

The following viewpoints are distinguished:

- The *stakeholder viewpoint* focuses on modeling the stakeholders, drivers, the assessments of these drivers, and the initial goals to address these drivers and assessments

- The *goal realization viewpoint* focuses on refining the initial, high-level goals into more concrete (sub-)goals using the aggregation relationship, and finally into requirements and constraints using the realization relationship

- The *goal contribution viewpoint* focuses on modeling and analyzing the influence relationships between goals (and requirements)

- The *principles viewpoint* focuses on modeling the relevant principles and the goals that motivate these principles

- The *requirements realization viewpoint* focuses on modeling the realization of requirements and constraints by means of core elements, such as actors, services, processes, application components, etc.

- The *motivation viewpoint* covers the entire motivational aspect and allows use of all motivational elements

All viewpoints are separately described below. For each viewpoint, its elements and relationships, the guidelines for its use, and its goal and target group are indicated. Furthermore, each viewpoint description contains example models. For more details on the goal and use of viewpoints, refer to Chapter 14 of [1].

C.2.1 Stakeholder Viewpoint

The stakeholder viewpoint allows the analyst to model the stakeholders, the internal and external drivers for change, and the assessments (in terms of strengths, weaknesses, opportunities, and threats) of these drivers. Also, the links to the initial (high-level) goals that address these concerns and assessments may be described. These goals form the basis for the requirements engineering process, including goal refinement, contribution and conflict analysis, and the derivation of requirements that realize the goals.

Table 36: Stakeholder Viewpoint Description

Stakeholder Viewpoint	
Stakeholders	Stakeholders, Business Managers, Enterprise and ICT Architects, Business Analysts, Requirements Managers
Concerns	Architecture mission and strategy, motivation
Purpose	Designing, deciding, informing
Scope	Motivation

Elements

- Stakeholder
- Driver
- Assessment

- Goal
- Outcome

C.2.2 Goal Realization Viewpoint

The goal realization viewpoint allows a designer to model the refinement of (high-level) goals into more tangible goals. The refinement of tangible goals into requirements or constraints, describe the properties that are then needed to realize the goals. The refinement of goals into sub-goals, is modeled using the aggregation relationship. The refinement of goals into requirements, is modeled using the realization relationship.

In addition, the principles may be modeled that guide the refinement of goals into requirements.

Table 37: Goal Realization Viewpoint Description

Goal Realization Viewpoint	
Stakeholders	Stakeholders, Business Managers, Enterprise and ICT Architects, Business Analysts, Requirements Managers
Concerns	Architecture mission, strategy and tactics, motivation
Purpose	Designing, deciding
Scope	Motivation

Elements

- Goal
- Principle
- Requirement
- Constraint
- Outcome

C.2.3 Requirements Realization Viewpoint

The requirements realization viewpoint allows the designer to model the realization of requirements by the core elements, such as business actors, business services, business processes, application services, application components, etc. Typically, the requirements result from the goal refinement viewpoint.

Additionally, this viewpoint can be used to refine requirements into more detailed requirements. The aggregation relationship is used for this purpose.

Table 38: Requirements Realization Viewpoint Description

Requirements Realization Viewpoint	
Stakeholders	Enterprise and ICT architects, business analysts, requirements managers
Concerns	Architecture strategy and tactics, motivation
Purpose	Designing, deciding, informing

Requirements Realization Viewpoint	
Scope	Motivation

Elements

- Goal
- Principle
- Requirement/constraint
- Outcome
- Value
- Meaning
- Core element
- Course of action
- Resource
- Capability
- Value stream

C.2.4   Motivation Viewpoint

The motivation viewpoint allows the designer or analyst to model the motivation aspect, without focusing on certain elements within this aspect. For example, this viewpoint can be used to present a complete or partial overview of the motivation aspect by relating stakeholders, their primary goals, the principles that are applied, and the main requirements on services, processes, applications, and objects.

Table 39: Motivation Viewpoint Description

Motivation Viewpoint	
Stakeholders	Enterprise and ICT Architects, Business Analysts, Requirements Managers
Concerns	Architecture strategy and tactics, motivation
Purpose	Designing, deciding, informing
Scope	Motivation

Elements

- Stakeholder
- Driver
- Assessment
- Goal
- Principle
- Requirement
- Constraint
- Outcome
- Value
- Meaning

C.3 Strategy Viewpoints

To describe strategic aspects of the enterprise, the viewpoints below have been defined. Each of these viewpoints presents a different perspective on modeling the high-level strategic direction and make-up of the enterprise that allows a modeler to focus on certain aspects. Therefore, each viewpoint considers only a selection of the elements and relationships that have been described in the preceding sections.

The following viewpoints are distinguished:

- The *strategy viewpoint* provides a high-level strategic overview of the strategies of the enterprise, its capabilities, value streams, and resources, and the envisaged outcomes

- The *capability map viewpoint* provides an overview of the capabilities of the enterprise

- The *value stream viewpoint* shows an overview of value-creating steps in the enterprise and the capabilities that support these

- The *outcome realization viewpoint* describes how high-level, business-oriented results are produced by the capabilities and resources of the enterprise

- The *resource map viewpoint* provides a structured overview of the resources of the enterprise

All viewpoints are separately described below. For each viewpoint, its elements and relationships, the guidelines for its use, and its goal and target group are indicated. For more details on the goal and use of viewpoints, refer to Chapter 14 of [1].

C.3.1 Strategy Viewpoint

The strategy viewpoint allows the Business Architect to model a high-level, strategic overview of the strategies (courses of action) of the enterprise, the capabilities, value streams, and resources supporting those, and the envisaged outcomes.

Table 40: Strategy Viewpoint Description

Strategy Viewpoint	
Stakeholders	CxOs, Business Managers, Enterprise and Business Architects
Concerns	Strategy development
Purpose	Designing, deciding
Scope	Strategy

Elements

- Course of action
- Capability
- Value stream
- Resource
- Outcome

C.3.2 Capability Map Viewpoint

The capability map viewpoint allows the Business Architect to create a structured overview of the capabilities of the enterprise. A capability map typically shows two or three levels of capabilities across the entire enterprise. It can be used as a heat map to identify areas of investment. In some cases, a capability map may also show specific outcomes delivered by these capabilities.

Table 41: Capability Map Viewpoint Description

Capability Map Viewpoint	
Stakeholders	Business Managers, Enterprise and Business Architects
Concerns	Architecture strategy and tactics, motivation
Purpose	Designing, deciding
Scope	Strategy

Elements

- Outcome
- Capability
- Resource

C.3.3 Value Stream Viewpoint

The value stream viewpoint allows the Business Architect to create a structured overview of a value stream, the capabilities supporting the stages in that value stream, the value created, and the stakeholders involved.

Table 42: Value Stream Viewpoint Description

Value Stream Viewpoint	
Stakeholders	Business Managers, Enterprise and Business Architects
Concerns	Architecture strategy and tactics, motivation
Purpose	Designing, deciding
Scope	Strategy

Elements

- Value stream
- Capability
- Outcome
- Stakeholder

C.3.4   Outcome Realization Viewpoint

The outcome realization viewpoint is used to show how the highest-level, business-oriented results are produced by the capabilities and underlying core elements.

Table 43: Outcome Realization Viewpoint Description

Outcome Realization Viewpoint	
Stakeholders	Business Managers, Enterprise and Business Architects
Concerns	Business-oriented results
Purpose	Designing, deciding
Scope	Strategy

Elements

- Capability
- Value stream
- Resource
- Outcome
- Value
- Meaning
- Core element

C.3.5   Resource Map Viewpoint

The resource map viewpoint allows the Business Architect to create a structured overview of the resources of the enterprise. A resource map typically shows two or three levels of resources across the entire enterprise. It can be used as a heat map to identify areas of investment. In some cases, a resource map may also show relationships between resources and the capabilities they are assigned to.

Table 44: Resource Map Viewpoint Description

Resource Map Viewpoint	
Stakeholders	Business Managers, Enterprise and Business Architects
Concerns	Architecture strategy and tactics, motivation
Purpose	Designing, deciding
Scope	Strategy

Elements

- Resource
- Capability
- Work package

C.4 Implementation and Migration Viewpoints

The following standard viewpoints for modeling implementation and migration aspects are distinguished:

- The *project viewpoint* is primarily used to model the management of architecture change

- The *migration viewpoint* is used to model the transition from an existing architecture to a target architecture

- The *implementation and migration viewpoint* is used to model the relationships between the programs and projects and the parts of the architecture that they implement

All viewpoints are described separately below. For each viewpoint the comprised elements and relationships, the guidelines for the viewpoint use, and the goal and target group of the viewpoint are indicated. Furthermore, each viewpoint description contains example models. For more details on the goal and use of viewpoints, refer to Chapter 14 of [1].

C.4.1 Project Viewpoint

A project viewpoint is primarily used to model the management of architecture change. The "architecture" of the migration process from an old situation (current state Enterprise Architecture) to a new desired situation (target state Enterprise Architecture) has significant consequences on the medium and long-term growth strategy and the subsequent decision-making process. Some of the issues that should be addressed by the models designed in this viewpoint are:

- Developing a fully-fledged organization-wide Enterprise Architecture is a task that may require several years

- All systems and services must remain operational regardless of the presumed modifications and changes of the Enterprise Architecture during the change process

- The change process may have to deal with immature technology standards (e.g., messaging, security, data, etc.)

- The change has serious consequences for the personnel, culture, way of working, and organization

Furthermore, there are several other governance aspects that might constrain the transformation process, such as internal and external cooperation, project portfolio management, project management (deliverables, goals, etc.), plateau planning, financial and legal aspects, etc.

Table 45: Project Viewpoint Description

Project Viewpoint	
Stakeholders	(Operational) Managers, Enterprise and ICT Architects, employees, shareholders
Concerns	Architecture vision and policies, motivation
Purpose	Deciding, informing
Scope	Implementation and Migration

Elements

- Goal
- Outcome
- Work package
- Implementation event
- Deliverable
- Business actor
- Business role

C.4.2   Migration Viewpoint

The migration viewpoint entails models and concepts that can be used for specifying the transition from an existing architecture to a desired architecture. Since the plateau and gap elements have been quite extensively presented in Chapter 12, here the migration viewpoint is only briefly described and positioned by means of Table 46.

Table 46: Migration Viewpoint Description

Migration Viewpoint	
Stakeholders	Enterprise Architects, Process Architects, Application Architects, Infrastructure Architects, Domain Architects, employees, shareholders
Concerns	History of models
Purpose	Designing, deciding, informing
Scope	Implementation and Migration

Elements

- Plateau
- Gap

C.4.3   Implementation and Migration Viewpoint

The implementation and migration viewpoint is used to relate programs and projects to the parts of the architecture that they implement. This view allows modeling of the scope of programs, projects, and project activities in terms of the plateaus that are realized or the individual architecture elements that are affected. In addition, the way the elements are affected may be indicated by annotating the relationships.

Furthermore, this viewpoint can be used in combination with the programs and projects viewpoint to support portfolio management:

- The programs and projects viewpoint is suited to relate business goals to programs and projects

  For example, this makes it possible to analyze at a high level whether all business goals are covered sufficiently by the current portfolio(s).

- The implementation and migration viewpoint is suited to relate business goals (and requirements) via programs and projects to (parts of) the architecture

  For example, this makes it possible to analyze potential overlap between project activities or to analyze the consistency between project dependencies and dependencies among plateaus or architecture elements.

Table 47: Implementation and Migration Viewpoint Description

Implementation and Migration Viewpoint	
Stakeholders	(Operational) Managers, Enterprise and ICT Architects, employees, shareholders
Concerns	Architecture vision and policies, motivation
Purpose	Deciding, informing
Scope	Multiple layers/Multiple aspects

Elements

- Goal
- Requirement
- Constraint
- Work package
- Implementation event
- Deliverable
- Plateau
- Gap
- Business actor
- Business role
- Location
- Core element

D Relationship to Other Standards, Specifications, and Guidance Documents

This appendix describes the relationship of the ArchiMate language to other standards and documents, including the TOGAF framework, the BIZBOK® Guide, UML, BPMN, and BMM™.

D.1 The TOGAF Framework

The ArchiMate language, as described in this standard, complements the TOGAF framework [4] in that it provides a vendor-independent set of concepts, including a graphical representation, that helps to create a consistent, integrated model "below the waterline", which can be depicted in the form of TOGAF views.

The structure of the ArchiMate core language closely corresponds with the three main architectures as addressed in the TOGAF ADM. The strategy, motivation, implementation, and migration elements approximately map onto the remainder of the ADM (although these elements may also be used in Phases B, C, and D). This is illustrated in Figure 116. This correspondence indicates a fairly easy mapping between TOGAF views and the ArchiMate viewpoints. A more detailed description of this correspondence is given in [6].

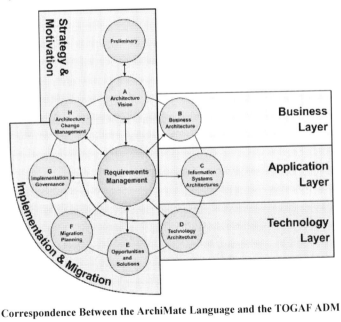

Figure 116: Correspondence Between the ArchiMate Language and the TOGAF ADM

Although some of the viewpoints that are defined in the TOGAF standard cannot easily be mapped onto ArchiMate viewpoints, the ArchiMate language and its analysis techniques support the concepts addressed in these viewpoints. While there is no one-to-one mapping between them, there is still a fair amount of correspondence between the ArchiMate viewpoints and the TOGAF viewpoints and many viewpoints from both address largely the same issues. Moreover, the viewpoint mechanism described in Section 13.4 lends itself well to define TOGAF viewpoints using ArchiMate concepts.

It is important to reiterate that the ArchiMate standard is a modeling language and not a framework. Therefore, the viewpoint definitions are more detailed and specify the stakeholders, concerns, level of detail, or abstraction level, and the entity types involved in the viewpoints. In the TOGAF Standard this is presented in a more general way. Therefore, some interpretation or transformation will be required.

In conclusion, the TOGAF and ArchiMate Standards can easily be used in conjunction:

- The two standards complement each other with respect to the definition of an architecture development process and the definition of an Enterprise Architecture modeling language

- The two standards overlap in their use of viewpoints, and the concept of an underlying common repository of architectural artifacts and models; i.e., they have a firm common foundation

- The combined use of the two standards can support a better communication with stakeholders

See [6] for a detailed explanation of how the TOGAF and ArchiMate Standards can be used together, including how to create a minimal ArchiMate based metamodel, which covers the whole ADM cycle.

D.2 The BIZBOK Guide

The ArchiMate language provides many concepts that are suitable for modeling Business Architectures. The core domains outlined in the BIZBOK Guide [18] – capabilities, value streams, organization, and information – are explicitly covered by relevant concepts in the Business Layer and strategy elements of the ArchiMate language. The other domains – stakeholders, strategies, policies, products, initiatives, and metrics – can also be described easily using appropriate ArchiMate concepts. The language supports key Business Architecture techniques such as capability mapping, organization mapping, information mapping, and value stream mapping, and with its extensive set of relationships it also covers the interconnections between these domains such as value stream – capability cross-mapping; e.g., see Example 21.

More advanced descriptions are also possible. In the TOGAF Series Guide: Value Streams [17] and the BIZBOK Guide, value streams are decomposed in a specific way. Stages in a value stream are not connected via relationships where value is exchanged, as in Example 21. Rather, the stages produce value items that are aggregated at a higher level into an overall value proposition, and the entry and exit conditions for each stage are specified explicitly. In the ArchiMate language, the former can be modeled with aggregation relationships and the latter using constraints.

D.3 The ArchiMate Language and Other Modeling Languages

The general approach in the design of the ArchiMate language is that it has some overlap with other modeling languages. Concepts that are shared between two languages can be used to bridge the gap and create integrated sets of models. This idea is illustrated in Figure 117.

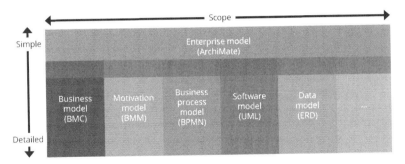

Figure 117: Correspondence Between the ArchiMate Language and Other Modeling Languages

This way, an ArchiMate model functions as a high-level "umbrella" that ties together different models at more detailed levels. From your Enterprise Architecture level, you can drill down into detailed models of specific aspects, and *vice versa*. The next sections illustrate this in more detail for the BPMN, UML, and BMM standards.

D.4   BPMN

Both the ArchiMate language and BPMN [12] can be used for modeling business processes. Their aims are different, however. ArchiMate notation is typically used for high-level processes and their relations to the enterprise context, but is not intended for detailed workflow modeling, whereas BPMN supports detailed sub-process and task modeling down to the level of executable specifications, but lacks the broader enterprise context, for example, to model the application services that support a process or the goals and requirements it has to fulfill.

Both languages share the concepts of (business) process and event. In the ArchiMate notation there is a single business process element that may be decomposed in other processes that are related using flow and triggering relationships, possibly using junctions to represent more complex connections. BPMN has a more fine-grained set of elements, with various types of events, tasks, and gateways. Its metamodel also distinguishes explicitly between process and sub-process (although it lacks a graphical representation of a business process itself). The BPMN concept of participant (or pool) and the ArchiMate concepts of business role or business actor (or application component for automated processes) also correspond.

In a typical scenario, both languages can be used in conjunction. Mapping from ArchiMate notation down to BPMN is fairly straightforward. The other way around loses the detailed elements of BPMN. Moreover, there are structural differences between the languages that preclude a direct concept-to-concept mapping and may merit a pattern-based approach. A detailed description of such a mapping is beyond the scope of this standard.

D.5   UML

The ArchiMate language has derived a number of concepts from UML [8]. For other concepts, straightforward correspondences can be defined.

In the Business Layer, the ArchiMate business process concept can be mapped onto UML activity diagrams, where more detailed specifications of such processes can be given (although BPMN would be the preferred language for detailed process and workflow modeling). The ArchiMate business actor and role concepts can both be mapped onto UML actors, although the latter can also be used for modeling automated actors. Business collaborations have been inspired by collaborations as defined in the UML standard [8], although the UML collaborations apply to components in the Application Layer.

In the Application Layer, the application component element corresponds to the UML component. This facilitates the direct linkage between higher-level Enterprise Architecture models described in ArchiMate notation and lower-level solution architecture and implementation models in UML in one continuous development chain. In a less direct manner, the ArchiMate application function concept can be mapped onto UML activity diagrams, and an application service to a use-case diagram. Application collaborations also correspond to UML collaborations.

Many of the elements of the ArchiMate Technology Layer correspond directly to UML. The node, artifact, device, system software, and path elements have a direct counterpart in UML (where system software is called execution environment).

In addition to these elements, many relationships in the ArchiMate language have close ties to UML as well. The ArchiMate association, composition, aggregation, specialization, and realization relationships have a direct counterpart in UML.

There are also some notable differences between the two languages. The ArchiMate serving relationship (formerly "used by") is different from UML dependency. Although their notations are similar, their directions are different. UML dependency is often used to model, for example, function calls in software programs, but in ArchiMate notation, the direction of the serving relationship denotes the direction of service delivery, independent of whether this service is called by the user or offered pro-actively by the provider. At the architectural level at which the ArchiMate language is aimed, the run-time operational details of such call graphs are less important than the more stable and generic notion of service provision.

This also points to another important difference: UML does not have a separate service concept, since in its object-oriented paradigm the behavior expressed by a service is encapsulated within the interface offering that behavior (i.e., its operations). The ArchiMate language differentiates between interfaces and the services they provide to allow, for example, specifying that the same service is offered through multiple interfaces. Hence, an ArchiMate application interface does not equate directly with a UML interface.

Finally, UML has a predefined, fixed set of diagram types, whereas the ArchiMate viewpoint mechanism allows for the construction of custom, stakeholder-oriented views on an architecture.

See [16] for a more detailed explanation about how the UML language and the ArchiMate standard can be used together.

D.6   BMM

The ArchiMate strategy and motivation elements have been inspired partly by the Business Motivation Model (BMM) [15]. BMM distinguishes between means, ends, and influencers and assessments. It provides fairly detailed concepts for these categories. The ArchiMate course of action element corresponds directly with the course of action element in BMM, whereas its directive concepts can be modeled with the ArchiMate principle, requirement, and constraint elements.

BMM concepts for modeling ends are typically mapped onto the ArchiMate goal element. Its influencers correspond to the ArchiMate element of driver, whereas its assessments map directly onto the ArchiMate assessment element.

Although a mapping between many of the ArchiMate motivation and implementation elements and BMM concepts is possible, BMM provides a more detailed, fine-grained description of business motivation. In that sense, it is comparable to the other languages described in this appendix. Where the ArchiMate language aims to cover a broad scope and interlink various domains, these more specialized languages zoom in on the details of their specific domains.

E   Changes from Version 2.1 to Version 3.2

E.1   Changes from Version 2.1 to Version 3.0.1

The main changes between Version 2.1 and Version 3.0.1 of the ArchiMate Specification are listed below. Note that this is not an exhaustive list; various smaller improvements have been made throughout the text of the document.

- Changed various definitions to increase alignment with the TOGAF framework

- Added an upper-level generic metamodel to explain the full structure of the language

- Restructured the set of relationships into structural, dynamic, dependency, and other relationships

- Allowed relationships to other relationships in some cases; e.g., to associate objects with flows or aggregate relationships within plateaus

- Improved the derivation of relationships

- Relaxed the constraints on relationships between layers in the ArchiMate core language

- Improved the grouping and junction concepts

- Renamed the "used by" relationship to "serving", in line with the other active names of relationships

- Changed the notation of the influence relationship for consistency with the other dependency relationships (access and serving)

- Introduced a directional notation for the assignment relationship by replacing the black circle at the "to" end by an arrow

- Added an optional notation to denote the layer of an element

  A letter M, S, B, A, T, P, or I in the top-left corner of an element can be used to denote a Motivation, Strategy, Business, Application, Technology, Physical, or Implementation & Migration element, respectively.

- Changed the notation of the representation and contract elements, to distinguish these from deliverable and business object, respectively

- Added events (with a time attribute) at all layers in the ArchiMate core language as well as to the implementation and migration elements

- Renamed the Motivation Extension to motivation elements and introduced a new outcome element

- Moved the value and meaning concepts from the Business Layer of the ArchiMate core language to the motivation elements

- Introduced new strategy elements for modeling the enterprise at a strategic level, notably capability, resource, and course of action

- Moved the location element to the generic metamodel

- Abolished the "required interface" notation

- Renamed the elements in the Technology Layer from infrastructure x to technology x

- Added application process, technology process, technology interaction, and technology collaboration, to increase the regularity of the layers

- Extended the Technology Layer with elements for modeling the physical world: facility, equipment, material, and distribution network

- Renamed the "communication path" element to "path" and extended its meaning, to integrate with the physical elements

- Improved the description of viewpoints and the viewpoints mechanism, removed the introductory viewpoint, and moved the basic viewpoints listed in the standard to an informative appendix to indicate they are intended as examples, not as a normative or exhaustive list

- Replaced the examples throughout the document

- Described the relationships of the ArchiMate standard with several other standards

- Created new tables of relationships based on the changes in the metamodel and derivation properties

ArchiMate 2.1 models are still mostly valid in ArchiMate 3.0.1. Two transformations may be applied to ensure conformance to the new version of the standard:

- Rename "used by" relationships to "serving"

- If a relationship between two elements in a model is no longer permitted (according to Appendix B), replace it by an association

  If it concerns an assignment of an application component to a business process or function, this may be replaced by a realization relationship from the application component to the business process or function. If it concerns an assignment of a location to another element, this may be replaced by an aggregation. In some cases, the modeler may want to replace the location by a facility.

E.2   Changes from Version 3.0.1 to Version 3.1

The main changes between Version 3.0.1 and Version 3.1 of the ArchiMate Specification are listed below. In addition to these changes, various other minor improvements in definitions and other wording have been made.

- Introduced a new strategy element: value stream

- Added an optional directed notation for the association relationship

- Improved the organization of the metamodel and associated figures

- Further improved and formalized the derivation of relationships

The formalization of the derivation rules as mentioned above has had a minor impact on the metamodel structure, since some relationships can now be derived that formerly had to be specified explicitly in the metamodel. It has also led to the removal of a small number of spurious relationships. To transform an ArchiMate 3.0.1 model to ArchiMate 3.1, any such relationship may be replaced by a directed association.

E.3 Changes from Version 3.1 to Version 3.2

The main changes between Version 3.1 and Version 3.2 of the ArchiMate Specification are listed below. In addition to these changes, various other minor improvements in definitions, explanations, and examples have been made.

- Improved the definitions of several concepts, most notably outcome, constraint, business function, and product

- Made the Physical elements part of the Technology Layer chapter instead of a separate chapter

- Changed the Technology Layer metamodel, making device, system software, facility, and equipment no longer subtypes of node but of technology internal active structure element, and adding composition and aggregation relationships with node.

- Added composition and aggregation relationships from plateau to outcome

- Added realization from material to equipment

- Improved the restrictions on derivation rules described in Section B.3.5

- Added a derivation rule for grouping

- Changed the icon notation of the meaning and communication network elements, added an icon notation for work package, and added new box notations for meaning, value, business object, contract, representation, work package, and deliverable

- Changed the default color of the plateau and gap elements to the same pink as the other Implementation and Migration elements

Acronyms

ABB	Architecture Building Block
ADM	Architecture Development Method (TOGAF framework)
ASCII	American Standard Code for Information Interchange
B2B	Business-to-Business
BMM	Business Motivation Model
BPMN	Business Process Model and Notation
CEO	Chief Executive Officer
CFO	Chief Financial Officer
CIO	Chief Information Officer
CMO	Chief Marketing Officer
CRM	Customer Relationship Management
ERD	Entity Relationship Diagram
GUI	Graphical User Interface
HTML	HyperText Markup Language
IoT	Internet of Things
JEE	Java, Enterprise Edition (was J2EE)
PDF	Portable Document Format
RTF	Rich Text Format
SBB	Solution Building Block
SLA	Service-Level Agreement
SWOT	Strengths, Weaknesses, Opportunities, and Threats
UML	Unified Modeling Language
WAN	Wide Area Network
WLAN	Wireless Local Area Network

Index

Made in the USA
Middletown, DE
10 February 2023

24497636R00117